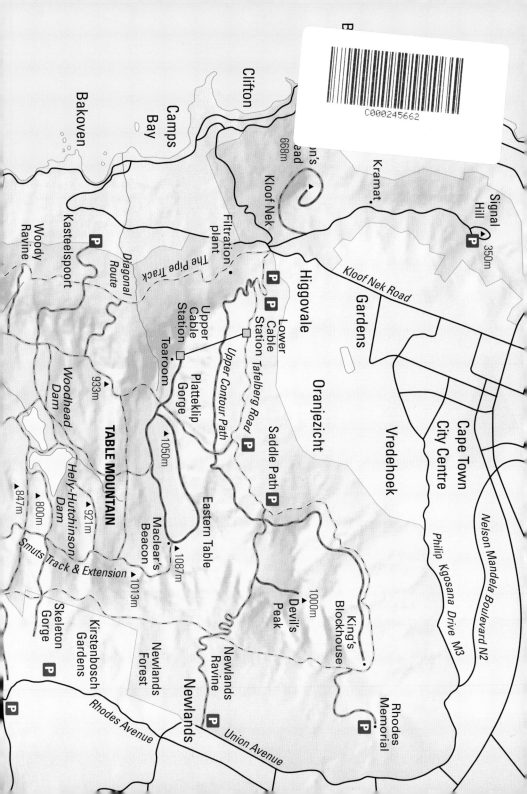

Quick ID Guide

# WILD FLOWERS
## OF THE CAPE PENINSULA

Hugh Clarke & Corinne Merry

Published by Struik Nature (an imprint of
  Penguin Random House South Africa (Pty)
  Ltd) Reg. No. 1953/000441/07
The Estuaries No. 4, Oxbow Crescent, Century
  City 7441
PO Box 1144, Cape Town, 8000 South Africa

Visit **www.penguinrandomhouse.co.za** and
  join the Struik Nature Club for updates,
  news, events and special offers.

First published in 2007 as *Common Wild
  Flowers of Table Mountain*
Second expanded edition published in 2013 as
  *Common Wild Flowers of Table Mountain &
  Silvermine*
Third expanded edition published in 2019

10 9 8 7 6 5 4 3 2 1

**Publisher:** Pippa Parker
**Editor:** Natalie Bell
**Designer:** Gillian Black
**Proofreader:** Thea Grobbelaar

Reproduction by Studio Repro and Hirt &
  Carter Cape (Pty) Ltd
Printed and bound in China by RR Donnelley

MIX
Paper from
responsible sources
FSC® C144853

PRINT: 978 1 77584 640 6
ePUB: 978 1 77584 641 3

**We are grateful to the Botanical
Society of South Africa for their
generous sponsorship.**

## Photographic credits

Photographs are labelled with the contributors' initials.
AB/WC = Abu Shawker, https://creativecommons.org/licenses/by-sa/3.0/deed.en;
BLS = Barrie Shoosmith; BM = Bruce Mackenzie; CM = Corinne Merry; CMcC = Claire
McCarthy; CW = Chris Walker; FS = Frankie Shoosmith; GN = Gregory Nicolson; HC = Hugh
Clarke; MA = Michael Archer; MB = Matt Buys; MN = Michael Nobel; SM = Sibyl Morris;
SR = Sheila Robinson; WPUJ = the late WPU Jackson, with permission from his daughter,
Rose Macmanus; ZG = Zane Godwin

**Front cover:** King Protea, *Protea cynaroides*, near Maclear's Beacon (CM)
**Back cover:** White Harveya, *Harveya capensis* (CM); Yellow Lobelia, *Monopsis lutea* (CM)
**Page facing title page:** White-eyed Roella, *Roella ciliata* (CM)
**Title page:** Cape Bogbean, *Villarsia manningiana* (CM)
**Contents page:** Hiker with King Proteas, *Protea cynaroides*, on Table Mountain (AB/WC)

**The authors and publisher of this book accept no responsibility for any loss, injury
or death sustained while using this book as a guide.**

# CONTENTS

# PREFACE

If you are keen to identify flowers while exploring the Cape Peninsula, and you like to 'put a name to a face', then this book is for you. It doesn't matter if you are a flower-lover, hiker, climber, tourist, or simply a person who appreciates beauty in nature. The text is written for absolute beginners and has been designed to make flower recognition and identification as easy as possible. A special effort has been made to record features that beginner flower-spotters are most likely to notice.

This book has evolved from two earlier editions: first came *Common Wild Flowers of Table Mountain*, with descriptions of about 200 flowers. Then we wrote *Common Wild Flowers of Table Mountain & Silvermine* with an additional 60 flowers. In this expanded third edition of this popular book, we describe a blooming 360 flowers, with the addition of flowers from Cape Point. We have also added new flower walks together with a map of Cape Point showing the new routes.

These three areas offer widely differing habitats and host a vast range of flower species:
- **Table Mountain** The flower-lover's 'must-see', whether you are going for a stroll in Newlands Forest or hiking up one of the many pathways that lead to a wonderland of fynbos flora.
- **Silvermine** Hike along the lower slopes or scramble up the rocky sections and look around at the scenic views of the city, the sea, and above all, the flora around you.
- **Cape Point** Walk along the coastline or cliffs to admire the view and see flowers rarely encountered elsewhere.

The diversity of plants in the Peninsula is mind-boggling and can be overwhelming. There are over 2,285 plant species here. Especially in the Summer months, the profusion of wild flowers is a joy to behold, made even better if you know what you are looking at!

We have put together some of the most popular walks around these three areas of the Cape Peninsula. The walking routes are plotted on three maps. The advantage of exploring the various footpaths is that the more areas you visit with differing habitats, the broader variety of flowers you will see. This area is a World Heritage Site, so please do not pick the flowers. Take only photographs and leave only footprints behind.

We hope this book will inspire you to explore the mountains and coastal areas, enjoy the magnificent scenery and identify for yourself the many beautiful flowers to be found.

**Hugh Clarke & Corinne Merry**

# ACKNOWLEDGEMENTS

Our thanks go firstly to Dr Bruce McKenzie, who vetted the botanical aspects of the text in the first edition, and to the other Bruce Mackenzie who co-authored the first two editions with us. Thank you to the many photographers listed on the imprint page. Frankie Shoosmith shared her knowledge of the flora of Cape Point, provided photographs and helped with the flower selection for Cape Point. We are extremely grateful to Peter Slingsby who generously provided us with a map of Cape Point when we needed it.

Our thanks also go to Pippa Parker and her capable staff, Gill Black and Natalie Bell, of Penguin Random House South Africa.

Corinne would like to thank her husband, Charles, and her other hiking companions, particularly Ineke Moseley, for being so patient during the many stops they made while she was photographing flowers.

Hugh would like to thank his wife, Fenja, for her support during the many hours spent compiling this work.

Any errors in the text or wrongful identifications are attributable entirely to the authors.

*Erica hirtiflora* blooming in Silvermine, with Fish Hoek and Simon's Town in the distance

CM

# INTRODUCTION

Table Mountain, Silvermine and Cape Point are three natural landmarks spanning the Cape Peninsula. They offer discrete natural habitats for diverse flora. Nowhere else in the world does an area of such beauty and rich biodiversity exist within a city inhabited by close to 3.8 million people.

Table Mountain is not only a World Heritage Site but, by global poll, it was voted as one of the world's Seven Wonders of Nature. It occupies an area of 57km$^2$, with 650km of hiking trails. Nearly one million people take the cable car each year to reach the top. The more adventurous hike to the summit or along the many hiking routes.

Silvermine lies south of Table Mountain. Although this protected conservation area is smaller than Table Mountain, its fynbos vegetation is rich in species. These include a surprisingly large number of endemics – species found nowhere else in the world – like the showy *Erica urna-viridis*, which only grows on the higher-lying areas of Silvermine East around Muizenberg Peak, or *Erica nevillei*, growing on Noordhoek

*Hymenolepis crithmifolia* hover in the foreground with Table Mountain standing behind

Peak in Silvermine West. Other attractions include some indigenous forests, caves and spectacular sea views over False Bay in the east, and Chapman's Peak Drive and Hout Bay in the west.

Cape Point is the southernmost tip of the Peninsula. The reserve has sea on three sides, towering stone cliffs with stunning vistas over the oceans and hosts over 1,000 flower species (14 of which are found nowhere else in the world). Over 270 bird species have made Cape Point their home. For flower-lovers, a walk in these wild areas is an amazing experience all year round, but especially during the Spring and Summer months (from September through to March).

We have selected flowers that are generally attractive, eye-catching and easily seen. Flowers that are really tiny and less interesting, which the average hiker or rambler would usually walk past without a second glance, are not featured. A few really beautiful species, although not widely dispersed, are included for interest and pleasure.

# HOW TO USE THIS BOOK

This book gives you a snapshot and description of 360 wild flowers that grow in the Cape Peninsula.

**(1) Colour tabs** on the side of each page help you to find the flower you wish to identify. The flowers are arranged according to colour. Try to match the flower you are looking at with the closest colour tab, then look at the flowers on those pages. (Sometimes there are colour variations in flowers, so you may have to look in the other colour sections for an elusive flower.)

**(2) Photographs** offer an instant ID. They are mostly close-ups, showing what you would see if you were right next to the flower. There are some inserts with a more distant view of the flowering plant.

We group flowers according to the predominant colour of their petals. We present the colour we found *most often* in the Cape Peninsula and we list other colour possibilities.

Flower colours can vary; you may find specimens of a lighter, darker or even a different shade from that in our photograph or description.

**(3) Flowering season** reflects the months in which we saw that species in bloom. Flowers may bloom outside these months, but if you have two lookalikes and one is not meant to be in flower at the time you are looking at it, this may help you to identify the species.

**(4) Height** is given in metres or centimetres. The maximum height of plants can vary according to their age, locality, frequency of fires, climatic variation and so on. We have followed the heights specified in reliable sources, moderated by our own observations in the Cape Peninsula.

**(5) Descriptions** follow the same sequence of headings: Leaves; Flower head; Distribution; Habitat. Text is simple; we have avoided complex botanical terms.

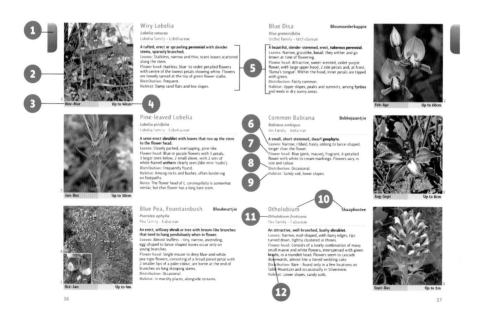

### Wiry Lobelia
*Lobelia setacea*
Lobelia family · Lobeliaceae

A tufted, erect or sprawling **perennial** with slender stems, sparsely branched.
**Leaves:** Stalkless, narrow and thin; scant leaves scattered along the stem.
**Flower head:** Hairless, blue- to violet-petalled flowers with centre of these violet petals showing white. Flowers are loosely spread at the top of green flower stalks.
**Distribution:** Frequent.
**Habitat:** Damp sand flats and low slopes.

Nov–Mar          Up to 40cm

### Pine-leaved Lobelia
*Lobelia pinifolia*
Lobelia family · Lobeliaceae

A semi-erect **shrublet** with leaves that run up the stem to the flower head.
**Leaves:** Closely packed, overlapping, pine-like.
**Flower head:** Blue or purple flowers with 5 petals, 3 larger ones below, 2 small above, with 2 sets of white-haired **anthers** clearly seen (like mini 'tusks').
**Distribution:** Frequently found.
**Habitat:** Among rocks and bushes, often bordering on footpaths.
**Notes:** The flower head of *L. coronopifolia* is somewhat similar, but that flower has a long bare stem.

Jan–Dec          Up to 50cm

### Blue Pea, Fountainbush          Bloukeurtjie
*Psoralea aphylla*
Pea family · Fabaceae

An erect, willowy shrub or tree with broom-like branches that tend to hang pendulously when in flower.
**Leaves:** Almost leafless – tiny, narrow, ascending, egg-shaped to lance-shaped leaves occur only on young branches.
**Flower head:** Single mauve to deep blue-and-white pea-type flowers, consisting of a broad joined petal with 2 smaller lips of a paler colour, are borne at the end of branches on long drooping stems.
**Distribution:** Occasional.
**Habitat:** In marshy places, alongside streams.

Oct–Jan          Up to 4m

### Blue Disa          Bloumoederkappie
*Disa graminifolia*
Orchid family · Orchidaceae

A beautiful, slender-stemmed, erect, **tuberous perennial**.
**Leaves:** Narrow, grasslike, basal; they wither and go brown at time of flowering.
**Flower head:** Attractive, sweet-scented, violet-purple flower, with large upper hood, 2 side petals and, at front, 'Duma's tongue'. Within the hood, inner petals are tipped with green.
**Distribution:** Fairly common.
**Habitat:** Upper slopes, peaks and summits, among **fynbos** and reeds in dry sunny areas.

Feb–Apr          Up to 60cm

### Common Babiana          Bobbejaantjie
*Babiana ambigua*
Iris family · Iridaceae

A small, short-stemmed, dwarf **geophyte**.
**Leaves:** Narrow, ribbed, hairy, oblong to lance-shaped, longer than the flower.
**Flower head:** Blue (pink, mauve), fragrant, 6-petalled flower with white to cream markings. Flowers vary in size and colour.
**Distribution:** Occasional.
**Habitat:** Sandy soil, lower slopes.

Aug–Sept          Up to 8cm

### Otholobium          Skaapbostee
*Otholobium fruticans*
Pea family · Fabaceae

An attractive, well-branched, bushy **shrublet**.
**Leaves:** Narrow, oval-shaped, with hairy edges, tips turned down, tightly clustered in threes.
**Flower head:** Consists of a lovely combination of many small mauve and white flowers, interspersed with green **bracts**, in a rounded head. Flowers seem to cascade downwards, almost like a tiered wedding cake.
**Distribution:** Rare – found only in a few locations on Table Mountain and occasionally in Silvermine.
**Habitat:** Lower slopes, sandy soils.

Sept–Dec          Up to 1m

36          37

**6** **Leaves** are described in terms of:
- size (large, small); leaf size is relative to flower size.
- shape (oval, round, sword-shaped); see the Illustrated Glossary on page 151.
- texture (rough, smooth) and
- where they are on the plant (high, low).

**7** **Flower head** describes the main features. Flower head can mean a dense cluster of tiny flowers, but our description refers to the overall impression of the head, not the tiny, individual blossoms.

**8** **Distribution** on the Peninsula is described as:
- **Rare** – found in only a few locations. Do not be disheartened if some wild flowers are described as 'Rare'. Not all flowers are widespread; some have very localized habitats. Although found only in a few locations, some appear prolifically, like the Red Disa (*Disa uniflora*) in the aqueduct area on Table Mountain. The Red Disa is rare in most localities, like Skeleton Gorge and Myburgh's Waterfall Ravine.
- **Occasional/Uncommon** – seen once in a while or somewhat irregularly
- **Fairly common** – seen regularly but not in abundance
- **Common** – often observed and widespread
- **Frequently found** – this term is used when a species is very common, widespread and abundant.

**9** **Habitat** is the likely place where each flower lives. Every plant has a preferred environment in which it thrives. Various factors like rainfall, altitude, soil type, wind and the amount of sunshine or shade determine a plant's habitat. Generally, the western and northern slopes of the Cape Peninsula are fairly dry, while eastern and southeastern slopes and mountain tops are high-rainfall areas.

**10** **Common names** for flowers have been given in English and Afrikaans, when possible. We recommend you learn the scientific names too, because a common name may refer to many different species.

**11** **Scientific names** are always in italics, with the genus first, followed by the species. This is the convention that botanists use to ensure they are speaking about the same plant. These formal names sometimes change, for scientific reasons.

**12** **Bold words** are defined in the Glossary on page 150.

**13** **Walking routes** are described in colour-coded tables, matching the routes plotted on the three maps, which are printed at the front and back of the book.

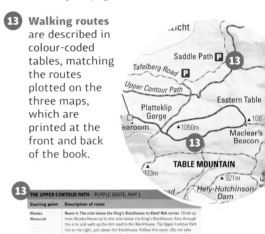

**13** THE UPPER CONTOUR PATH – PURPLE ROUTE, MAP 1

| Starting point | Description of route |
|---|---|
| Rhodes Memorial | Route 4: The stile below the King's Blockhouse to Kloof Nek corner  Climb up from Rhodes Memorial to the stile below the King's Blockhouse. Pass through the stile and walk up the dirt road to the Blockhouse. The Upper Contour Path lies to the right, just above the Blockhouse. Follow this route. (Do not take the path that goes straight up.) The Upper Contour Path runs parallel to Tafelberg Road, about 180m above it. It ends at the entrance to Kloof Nek Waterworks, just above Kloof Nek corner. |

**The Upper Slopes and the Back Table**

These paths are marked in orange on Map 1. There is no definitive starting point for these walks.

The Back Table, about 750m above sea level, is criss-crossed with numerous footpaths. Many hiking routes are possible, as described in the box below.

This large area encompasses a wide variety of habitats: wet, south-facing rock faces; flat, damp areas alongside the dams, flat, rocky outcrops; bushy areas and dry, open slopes. Each supports particular flowering plants, including proteas, disas, ericas, daisies and irises.

Once you are up the mountain, the four major routes are:
- Smuts Track (east)
- Apostles Path (west)
- numerous paths around the dams (centre)
- paths towards the Front Table.

*Hikers taking a break on the Back Table overlooking Hely-Hutchinson Dam*

**13** THE UPPER SLOPES AND THE BACK TABLE   ORANGE ROUTES, MAP 1

| Starting point | Description of route |
|---|---|
| Kirstenbosch | Route 5: Smuts Track and/or its extension  Smuts Track is a steep walk up Skeleton Gorge with some easy rock scrambling and ladders. At the top, turn right to Maclear's Beacon, the highest point on the mountain. |
| Western side of mountain | Route 6: Apostles Path  This runs from Platteklip Gorge in the north to Grootkop, Judas Peak and Suikerbossie in the south. This is the drier side of the mountain. |
| The dams | Route 7: Back Table  An easy way to see all the dams is to walk up the Bridle Path and follow it past De Villiers, Alexandra and Victoria dams to the main dams, Woodhead and Hely-Hutchinson. |
| Between the dams and the Front Table | Route 8: Back Table to Front Table  There are a number of linking paths on the western, central and eastern sides, between the dams and the Front Table. These are clearly shown on the map. |

15

Cape Point in the distance with Paulsberg looming picturesquely on the right

# HOW TO FIND THE FLOWERS

The best strategy to increase your chances of finding different flowers is to walk along different routes. These are some of our favourite flower walks. Maps of the routes are at the front and back 'of the book for quick and easy reference.

Visit as many habitats as you can: kloofs, streams or **seeps**, open areas, rocky outcrops, sandy areas, high altitudes, low altitudes, the sunny western side and the wetter eastern side.

Different flowers grow at different times, so repeating the same routes as the seasons change offers different flower-spotting possibilities.

In the flowering season (August to March), you could see 50–100 of the flowers in this book – *in a day*. If you walk frequently on various parts of the Peninsula, you could see most of the flowers in this book – *in a year*. You will also see other flowers, not just those described. Even during the worst months, Bruce Mackenzie recorded sightings of over 100 flowering species – *in a month*.

Fire triggers growth in many plants, so you should hunt for flowers in recently burnt areas to find 'specials'. Fire plays an integral role in fynbos and most species are adapted to withstand it; some are dependent on it for flowering.

When you plan your flower-spotting walks, consider the distance and timing of the walk. In many cases, you will have to make a return trip, so factor this into your planning.

## USEFUL INFORMATION

**MY GREEN CARD AND THE WILD CARD**
SANParks website gives details of My Green Card and the Wild Card. If you live in Cape Town, you are entitled to purchase My Green Card. This card grants free entry to Silvermine, Cape Point, Boulders and Oudekraal, for you and up to five other South Africans with you at the time. To purchase, you will need to present your ID, proof of residence and 2 passport photographs. A total of 12 entries is available on this card. It is valid for one year. A Wild Card gives access to South African National Parks.

**MAPS**
The maps in this book are a general guide. We recommend these detailed maps by Peter Slingsby:
- Table Mountain
- Silvermine & Hout Bay
- Cape Point, Simon's Town, Fish Hoek.
Slingsby maps are the only maps endorsed by the Table Mountain National Park and approved by the Mountain Club of South Africa.
**https://slingsby-maps.myshopify.com**

# WALKING ROUTES

These flower walking routes are in three main areas in the Table Mountain National Park: Table Mountain, Silvermine and Cape Point. Walkers should read the descriptions of these walking routes in conjunction with the maps provided.

## TABLE MOUNTAIN

Table Mountain offers a variety of walks for different abilities and fitness levels. The walks are colour-coded in the tables on the following pages, from easy yellow routes to more arduous red routes. Choose the walk you wish to do, then use the colour in the description to help you find the corresponding route on the map.

### The Contour Paths

There are two contour paths: an upper and a lower. Both paths offer easy mountain walks.

| THE LOWER CONTOUR PATH – YELLOW ROUTES, MAP 1 | |
| --- | --- |
| **Starting point** | **Description of route** |
| Constantia Nek parking area | **Route 1: Constantia Nek to Devil's Peak**  Begin at the Table Mountain National Park sign, on the northern side of the traffic circle. Walk along the dirt road; keep left at the first fork. Do not take any further turns. This eventually becomes a well-marked footpath that runs above Kirstenbosch Gardens.<br><br>When you reach Kirstenbosch, consider visiting the upper reaches of these world-famous gardens, as there is a superb display of **fynbos**, including flowers you will not find on Table Mountain.<br><br>From Kirstenbosch, the path continues round the base of Devil's Peak, along an indigenous forest path with boardwalks. It is shady and cool in Summer. Walk until you come to a stile just below the King's Blockhouse. As you leave the forest, you will come across flowers that enjoy this good rainfall area. In season, you can see pelargoniums, irises and daisies in a grassy open area around Rhodes Memorial. |

Hikers admiring the *Disa uniflora* along the Disa River, near the Hely-Hutchinson Dam

| Starting point | Description of route |
| --- | --- |
| Rhodes Memorial | **Route 2: Devil's Peak to Kloof Nek corner** Climb up from Rhodes Memorial to the stile below the King's Blockhouse. Pass through the stile then walk down the dirt road. (Do not go up to the Blockhouse.) This road takes you around Devil's Peak to the front of the mountain. It becomes a tarred road, Tafelberg Road, that runs past the Cable Station to Kloof Nek corner. This slope of the mountain basks in full sunshine and has few trees, except for a number of Cork Oaks growing just below Woodstock Cave.<br><br>The Upper Contour Path is a good alternative if you don't want to walk on the road. (See the purple route on the map.) |
| Kloof Nek parking area | **Route 3: The Pipe Track** At Kloof Nek corner, opposite the Table Mountain Cableway parking area, a Table Mountain National Park signboard indicates the starting point of the Pipe Track. It runs along the drier side of the mountain, below buttresses called the Twelve Apostles. The track heads southwards to the bottom of Oudekraal Ravine, where it turns up towards the Twelve Apostles. Several ascents begin from the Pipe Track.<br><br>This is a rewarding area in terms of wild flowers. In the height of Summer, brilliant purple-pink pelargoniums splash the mountainside with colour. The first part of the track also hosts an annual display of the bright yellow Conebush (*Leucospermum conocarpodendron*). |

On the Pipe Track near Kasteelspoort

## THE UPPER CONTOUR PATH – PURPLE ROUTE, MAP 1

| Starting point | Description of route |
| --- | --- |
| Rhodes Memorial | **Route 4: The stile below the King's Blockhouse to Kloof Nek corner** Climb up from Rhodes Memorial to the stile below the King's Blockhouse. Pass through the stile and walk up the dirt road to the Blockhouse. The Upper Contour Path lies to the right, just above the Blockhouse. Follow this route. (Do not take the path that goes straight up.) The Upper Contour Path runs parallel to Tafelberg Road, about 180m above it. It ends at the entrance to Kloof Nek Waterworks, just above Kloof Nek corner. |

## The Upper Slopes and the Back Table

These paths are marked in orange on Map 1. There is no definitive starting point for these walks.

The Back Table, about 750m above sea level, is criss-crossed with numerous footpaths. Many hiking routes are possible. This large area encompasses a wide variety of habitats: wet, south-facing rock faces; flat, damp areas alongside the dams; flat, rocky outcrops; bushy areas and dry, open slopes. Each supports particular flowering plants, including proteas, disas, ericas, daisies and irises. **Once you are up the mountain, the four major routes are:**

- Smuts Track (east)
- Apostles Path (west)
- numerous paths around the dams (centre)
- paths towards the Front Table.

Hikers taking a break on the Back Table overlooking Hely-Hutchinson Dam

## THE UPPER SLOPES AND THE BACK TABLE – ORANGE ROUTES, MAP 1

| Starting point | Description of route |
| --- | --- |
| Kirstenbosch | **Route 5: Smuts Track and/or its extension** Smuts Track is a steep walk up Skeleton Gorge with some easy rock scrambling and ladders. At the top, turn right to Maclear's Beacon, the highest point on the mountain. |
| Western side of mountain | **Route 6: Apostles Path** This runs from Platteklip Gorge in the north to Grootkop, Judas Peak and Suikerbossie in the south. This is the drier side of the mountain. |
| Constantia Nek parking area | **Route 7: Dams on the Back Table** From the parking area, walk along the dirt road; keep left at the first fork and walk up the Bridle Path. Continue past De Villiers, Alexandra and Victoria dams to Woodhead and Hely-Hutchinson. |
| Between the dams and the Front Table | **Route 8: Back Table to Front Table** There are a number of linking paths on the western, central and eastern sides, between the dams and the Front Table. |

## The Top Table and the summits

These paths are marked in red on Map 1 and require a moderate degree of fitness.

The simplest and quickest way to get to the top of the mountain is by cable car, but you won't see any of the lower-altitude flowers that way. Once at the top, you have a wide variety of routes to explore in search of flowers. Altitude has an impact on the flowers that grow here. High up, the weather can be harsh: it is colder, wetter and much windier than on the more protected lower slopes and, as a result, the plants on the Front Table are mainly tough, wiry-stemmed reeds, with relatively few flowering shrubs visible.

Although there are some lovely flowers on the Top Table (red routes), flower-spotters will see more by walking down to the lower areas, such as the Back Table (orange routes) or the more sheltered lower slopes (yellow routes).

The highest peaks have superb views but their climate does not support a huge variety of plants; we recommend the Back Table or lower routes for flower-spotting.

| MOUNTAIN TOPS – RED ROUTES, MAP 1 | |
|---|---|
| **Starting point** | **Description of route** |
| Various | **Route 9: Optional routes** The walks on the higher reaches of Table Mountain and the ascents of Devil's Peak, Grootkop and Lion's Head are shown in red on the map. |

Up Devil's Peak, with blue *Aristea bakeri*, yellow *Bobaria indica* and pink *Watsonia borbonica*

Hikers on the drier Apostles Path route

## The ascents

These paths are marked in green on Map 1. There are 13 fairly commonly used ascents to the top of the mountain. Always stick to the clear, easily recognizable paths.

The ascents, usually via gorges or ravines, provide shadier, cooler and more sheltered habitats. They are often forested and punctuated by streams.

> **!** The ascents marked with an exclamation mark are not recommended unless you know the mountain well or have a good map or guide.

| THE ASCENTS – GREEN ROUTES, MAP 1 | |
|---|---|
| **Starting point** | **Description of route** |
| Constantia Nek parking area | **Route 10: Bridle Path**  Start at the signboard for the Table Mountain National Park. Follow the dirt road. Keep left at the first fork. At the next fork, take a sharp left turn. Follow this road past an iron bridge to the dams on the Back Table. |
| Cecilia Forest parking | **Route 11: Cecilia Forest (Spilhaus Ravine)**  Park at Cecilia Forest parking area. Walk up the dirt road from the parking. Turn first right. Walk straight along, ignoring a left turn, until you reach a pathway next to a stream (that may be dry). Turn left; walk up this path. It crosses a dirt road at a hairpin corner and continues upwards. Follow it upwards until just before it joins the Constantia Nek route. Turn left to return to your starting point. |
| Rycroft Gate (Gate 3) at Kirstenbosch Garden Centre | **Route 12: Nursery Ravine (from Kirstenbosch Gardens)**  Begin at the top gate to Kirstenbosch Gardens on Rhodes Drive. Follow the brick-paved road through the gardens to the Contour Path. The route is well marked. Follow the sign to Nursery Ravine. Hike upwards. |
| Gate 2 at Kirstenbosch Garden Centre | **Route 13: Skeleton Gorge (from Kirstenbosch Gardens)**  There are a number of footpaths leading from Kirstenbosch Gardens to Skeleton Gorge that are well signposted. Ask at the entrance for directions if in any doubt. There are ladders halfway up the gorge. This is a well-used route with easy rock scrambling. Take care as it is slippery when wet. |

CM

Smuts Track above Skeleton Gorge rewards walkers with panoramic views

| Starting point | Description of route |
|---|---|
| Newlands Forest Station | **Route 14: Newlands Ravine** Park at Newlands Forest parking area. Walk up the tarred path and turn left at the top. Just past the stream, take the footpath upwards and continue until you reach a dirt road. Turn right, and almost immediately take the hairpin bend left. Follow this road until you come to the Contour Path sign. Once you reach the Contour Path, turn right. About a kilometre further on, there is a picnic table: the ascent path is on your left. |
| Saddle Path parking area | **Route 15: Saddle Path from Tafelberg Road** Drive along Tafelberg Road past the Cable Station. Continue past Platteklip Gorge. Drive on for about another kilometre. You will find limited parking on the left. The start of the ascent is clearly marked. This is a straightforward climb to the saddle between Devil's Peak and Table Mountain. |
| Platteklip parking area | **Route 16: Platteklip Gorge** The Platteklip parking area is just over a kilometre from the Cable Station, travelling in the direction of Devil's Peak. The ascent is a straightforward slog to the top. Once at the top, turn left to go to Maclear's Beacon or right to go to the Upper Cable Station. |
| Kloof Nek parking area | **Route 17: Diagonal Route** Walk along the Pipe Track for a few kilometres until you reach the Diagonal Route sign on your left. Although this route is safe, it is better to walk this with someone who knows the way to the top. |
| Theresa Avenue, Camps Bay | **Route 18: Kasteelspoort** There is limited parking between 25 and 27 Theresa Avenue, Camps Bay. This starting point can be used for ascents on the western side of the mountain. Take the road leading up to the Pipe Track. When you meet the Pipe Track, turn left until you come to the Kasteelspoort sign. |

| Starting point | Description of route |
| --- | --- |
| Theresa Avenue, Camps Bay | **Route 19: Woody Ravine** There is limited parking between 25 and 27 Theresa Avenue, Camps Bay. This starting point can be used for ascents on the western side of the mountain. Take the road leading up to the Pipe Track. When you reach the Pipe Track, bear right until you come to the Woody Ravine sign. |
| Theresa Avenue, Camps Bay | **Route 20: Corridor Ravine** There is limited parking between 25 and 27 Theresa Avenue, Camps Bay. This starting point can be used for ascents on the western side of the mountain. Take the road leading up to the Pipe Track. When you reach the Pipe Track, bear right until you come to the Woody Ravine sign. From Woody Ravine, continue along the path, cross the Slangolie Ravine stream and proceed up through trees and around the buttress until you reach a fork in the path. Take the left turn to begin the ascent. |
| ! • Theresa Avenue, Camps Bay | **Route 21: Oudekraal Ravine** There is limited parking between 25 and 27 Theresa Avenue, Camps Bay. This starting point can be used for ascents on the western side of the mountain. Take the road leading up to the Pipe Track. When you reach the Pipe Track, bear right until you come to the Woody Ravine sign. Continue on the path. Cross the Slangolie Ravine stream. From the bottom of Corridor Ravine, continue straight along a winding path for about a kilometre until the path turns left and starts ascending Oudekraal Ravine. This path is not well maintained. |
| ! • Ruyterplaats, Hout Bay | **Route 22: Llandudno Ravine** Park outside Ruyterplaats, just before turning left to the Suikerbossie Restaurant. The ascent, while safe, is not described here and should only be attempted with someone who knows the way. |

# SILVERMINE

The Silvermine section of the Table Mountain National Park lies on a plateau at the top of Ou Kaapse Weg (translation from Afrikaans is 'Old Cape Road'). This road forms a neat division between Silvermine West and Silvermine East. The Silvermine map shows some of the more popular routes in orange. Other easy walking routes are shown in light brown. Ascent routes are shown in green. The high peaks or steep climbs are shown in red. The yellow sections are the lower contour paths that are generally easily walked. This is just a small sample of the many hiking paths in this area.

## Silvermine West

The western side of Silvermine lies on the Table Mountain side of Ou Kaapse Weg. There are stunning views of the Atlantic coast from the higher peaks. In Summer, the southern slopes of Constantiaberg can turn white when *Erica lutea* and *Erica mammosa* are in full bloom, while in Spring, the area glows bright yellow with the Sickleleaf Conebush (*Leucadendron xanthoconus*) and the eastern slopes showcase the bright pink *Erica abietina* subsp. *constantiana*.

### ENTRANCE TIMES
07:00–18:00 (exit by 19:00)  October to April
08:00–17:00 (exit by 18:00)  May to September

### ENTRANCE FEES
**SILVERMINE WEST:** Entrance fees are payable. You may use a My Green Card or a Wild Card for free entry.
**SILVERMINE EAST:** Entrance is free.

*Xiphotheca fruticosa* in the foreground with Silvermine Dam and the South Peninsula behind

CM

Views from Constantiaberg, looking over Chapman's Peak, with *Protea speciosa* in the foreground

## WESTERN PLATEAU ROUTES – ORANGE ROUTES, MAP 2

| Starting point | Description of route |
| --- | --- |
| Silvermine Gate 1 | **Route 1: The River Walk** Park near Entrance Gate 1. Follow the path, which is shady and cool in Summer and has boardwalks in places, until it reaches Silvermine Dam. Alternatively, the walk can be done in reverse: park your vehicle in the parking area near the Silvermine Dam. Walk back towards Entrance Gate 1. The return trip can be a walk along the road unless a second car is used. |
| Silvermine Dam parking area | **Route 2: Elephant's Eye and Constantiaberg** Follow the Jeep track to the right of the dam, staying left at the first junction. Continue up a winding road. At the top of the rise, take the path to the right. Before you reach the Tokai Fire Lookout, turn left. Higher up, take a path to the right to go to Elephant's Eye Cave, or continue left to the top of Constantiaberg (928m) where there are superb views in all directions. Your return path starts near the southwesterly corner of the fence around the mast. It takes you to the top of Blackburn Ravine. Turn left here and follow the footpath that joins the Jeep track, returning you to the start. Constantiaberg summit is marked as red on the map. |
| Silvermine Dam parking area | **Route 3: Noordhoek Circuit** This is an easy walk along the Jeep track, with excellent views from Noordhoek Peak. Begin your walk below the dam wall and stay on this Jeep track. When you are near the peak, turn left and walk along a short path leading to the summit. Be careful in strong wind. Return to the Jeep track and continue your clockwise circuit until you reach a fork in the track. Take the right-hand path back to your car. |

Bokkop in central Silvermine with *Ursinia paleacea* in the foreground

## The western ascents

Only the Old Wagon Road route begins from Ou Kaapse Weg. The rest of the walks climb up to the Silvermine plateau from Chapman's Peak Drive.

| THE ASCENTS – GREEN ROUTES, MAP 2 | |
| --- | --- |
| **Starting point** | **Description of route** |
| Ou Kaapse Weg (southern end) | **Route 4: Old Wagon Road** Park in the parking area ±400m from the Silvermine Road intersection. It is on the northwest side of the road. Follow a Jeep track up to the parking area at the Gate 1 entrance to the reserve (western side). |
| Chapman's Peak Drive (East Fort parking) | **Route 5: Chapman's Peak** Park at the East Fort parking on Chapman's Peak Drive. The route follows the Jeep track into Blackburn Ravine. Cross the river and follow the path south. This path climbs for a while then traverses the slopes below the band of rock and eventually arrives at the neck between Chapman's Peak and Noordhoek Peak. At the path intersection, go straight. (Alternatively, take the path to the right, which takes you down to the road where you may park a second vehicle.) You will skirt Lower Chapman's Peak and then climb up to Chapman's Peak (593m) for superb views all around. Return the same way. Chapman's Peak summit is marked as red on the map. |
| Chapman's Peak Drive (East Fort parking) | **Route 6: Blackburn Ravine** Park at the East Fort parking on Chapman's Peak Drive. Walk up past the old fort and zigzag along the Jeep track. Near Blackburn Kloof take the upper fork. Cross the river a bit higher up the slope. Follow the path to the top of Blackburn Ravine. |
| Chapman's Peak Drive (near top) | **Route 7:Ascent to Silvermine Plateau** The path starts beyond the toll plaza (driving south) at a left-hand parking loop. Walk uphill. When you reach the intersection, you have three choices: turning right takes you to Chapman's Peak; turning left takes you to Blackburn Ravine and down to the road. Going straight will take you up to Silvermine Plateau – a long, steep climb. |

## Silvermine East

Silvermine East is on the Muizenberg side of Ou Kaapse Weg. It offers superb views of the False Bay coast from many vantage points. In Summer, the area becomes a kaleidoscope of colour: bright yellow flowers from various Aspalathus bushes, pink Ericas in abundance, the blue shrub *Psoralea pinnata* and the pink-flowered tree *Virgilia oroboides* lining streams, while the white-flowered *Syncarpha vestita* creates snow-like patches in areas.

| EASTERN PLATEAU ROUTES – ORANGE ROUTES, MAP 2 | |
| --- | --- |
| **Starting point** | **Description of route** |
| Silvermine Gate 2 | **Route 8: Amphitheatre and Kalk Bay Peak**  Begin at the parking area close to Entrance Gate 2. Walk along the Jeep track in a southeasterly direction, past a large sign with a map. At the first road intersection, turn right. As soon as you have crossed the river, turn left onto a footpath. When this meets another Jeep track, turn left and very soon thereafter turn right onto a path that takes you south to the Amphitheatre. Keep left at the intersection and follow the path to Kalk Bay Peak (516m). Continue walking for some distance to a second beacon where there are superb views over False Bay. A descent followed by a more level path brings you back to the Jeep track. Turn left and follow this to your starting point. |

*Disa ferruginea* blooms between the boulders near Steenberg Peak

| Starting point | Description of route |
|---|---|
| Silvermine Gate 2 | **Route 9: Higher Steenberg Peak**  Begin at the parking area close to Entrance Gate 2. Walk along the Jeep track in a southeasterly direction, past a large sign with a map. Simply follow this Jeep track; do not turn right at any intersection. The track turns left, going north, shortly after Junction Pool. At the next intersection, turn left onto a footpath. Follow this to the peak (537m), then continue westwards and down a stepped path to get back to the Jeep track, which will bring you back to your starting point. |
| Silvermine Gate 2 | **Route 10: Two Pools Circuit**  Begin at the parking area close to Entrance Gate 2. Walk along the Jeep track in a southeasterly direction, past a large sign with a map. Keep left. When you reach the second intersection, Junction Pool is ahead of you, on your right (it dries up in Summer). Turn right. Head south. You will pass Nellie's Pool on your left. Continue for a short distance until you come to an information hub. Turn right and follow the Jeep track, which takes you back to your starting point. |

## The eastern ascents
These walks climb up to the Steenberg Plateau from Boyes Drive.

| THE ASCENTS – GREEN ROUTES, MAP 2 | |
|---|---|
| **Starting point** | **Description of route** |
| Boyes Drive (Lakeside, northern end) | **Route 11: Steenberg Plateau**  Park on Boyes Drive near the Steenberg Plateau sign. Walk up a steep path to the top. You can either turn left to Muizenberg Peak (507m) or continue walking straight to the Jeep track. From that point there are several routes to explore.. |
| Boyes Drive (Muizenberg) | **Route 12: Peck's Valley**  Park on Boyes Drive near the Peck's Valley sign. Begin your walk at an opening in the stone wall. Ascend to the Contour Path, turn right, and continue to the top of the plateau. At the junction, go right to Muizenberg Peak or left towards St James Peak (422m). |
| Boyes Drive (just past Muizenberg, heading south) | **Route 13: Bailey's Kloof**  Park on Boyes Drive near the Shark Spotters' shelter. There is a Bailey's Kloof sign. Walk straight up. At the intersection on top, go right to ascend St James Peak or straight for Mimetes Valley. |
| Boyes Drive (at S-bend with Oukraal sign) | **Route 14: Old Mule Path and Spes Bona**  Park on Boyes Drive near the Oukraal sign. Go left along the ascending path. At the junction, turn right and follow the Jeep track. At the next junction, turn left up the slope towards the indigenous forest. At the head of the valley, turn left for the Amphitheatre or right for Kalk Bay Peak. |
| Boyes Drive (southern end) | **Route 15: Echo Valley**  Park on Boyes Drive near the Echo Valley sign. Climb into the valley without turning off the path. The upper end is home to the indigenous and curiously named Amazon Forest. At the top, turn right for the Amphitheatre or continue around Klein-Tuinkop. |

Summit of Paulsberg with Vasco de Gama Peak and Cape Point in the distance

## CAPE POINT

Cape Point is the southernmost point of the Table Mountain National Park and the Peninsula. The eight flower walks included here have been chosen for the variety of flowers they offer the walker. Most of these routes criss-cross the plateau because the beach walks are not so floriferous. An exception is the walk from Platboom to Gifkommetjie, which traverses dunes and coastal scrub. This walk presents *Euphorbia caput-medusae* and plenty of *Aspalathus carnosa*. In Summer, on the higher ground near Sirkelsvlei, you can see a white carpet of *Syncarpha vestita*, which looks like snow, hence its common name, Cape Snow.

For those who have time, Cape Point boasts a two-day hike right around the reserve, with overnight accommodation in three huts near Rooikrans, named after plants: Erica, Restio and Protea. A western section of the hike leads across private property, which the owners allow only the overnight hikers to use. This two-day hike will reveal the full spectrum of flowers to be seen at any one time.

Please note that most of the walks described are one-way, so you will need to leave a car at each end or return the way you came. The exception is the walk from Olifantsbos to Sirkelsvlei, where the return journey is along a different route.

### ENTRANCE TIMES

06:00–18:00 October to March
07:00–17:00 April to September

### ENTRANCE FEES

A fee is payable to enter Cape Point Nature Reserve. You may use a My Green Card or a Wild Card for free entry.

## CAPE POINT FLOWER WALKS – YELLOW ROUTES, MAP 3

| Starting point | Description of route |
|---|---|
| Smitswinkel viewpoint, close to Entrance Gate | **Route 1: False Bay Coast (northern section)** Take the path leading south from the parking area. Walk around the base of Paulsberg. You will see a path going up the peak – this optional detour is well worth the effort. Continue south to the Old Cannon at Kanonkop. At the cannon, you can either take the left-hand fork to go down to the parking area at Booi se Skerm, or take the right-hand fork to go to the Buffelsfontein Visitor Centre. |

The endemic *Staavia dodii* near Olifantsbos in Cape Point

| Starting point | Description of route |
|---|---|
| Buffelsfontein Visitor Centre parking area | **Route 2: Kanonkop** The walk begins at the Visitor Centre. Cross the road that heads to Bordjiesrif parking area. Walk on the path heading north to Kanonkop. When you reach the cannon, you can either take the route that drops down to Booi se Skerm on the coast (where you can park a second vehicle) or return along the same route. |
| Buffelsfontein Visitor Centre parking area | **Route 3: False Bay Coast (southern section)** Walk south from the Visitor Centre. Keep right where the path forks and stick to this trail, which keeps you well above the coast. You will have a view into the tidal cave, Antoniesgat, before you arrive at the Rooikrans parking area. |
| Rooikrans parking area | **Route 4: Vasco de Gama Peak** Ascend the path from the parking area. As you climb, you will notice turn-offs to the overnight huts. Continue straight, almost to the peak, before the path leads down to the restaurant and funicular parking area. |
| Restaurant parking area (northwest corner) | **Route 5: Cape of Good Hope** From the southern side of the parking area, descend through the fynbos to the cliffs overlooking Dias Beach. A worthwhile detour takes you down wooden stairs to Dias Beach. Continue walking on the path along the cliffs to the Cape Maclear viewpoint. From here, you can walk down to the Cape of Good Hope. |

| Starting point | Description of route |
| --- | --- |
| Platboom parking area | **Route 6: Coastal walk to Gifkommetjie (West Coast, southern section)** This walk begins in the Platboom parking area and takes you through coastal dune vegetation. The path is not always obvious, but the turning leading up to the parking area at Gifkommetjie is signposted. This is the only uphill on the walk. |
| Olifantsbos parking area | **Route 7: Sirkelsvlei Circular Route (West Coast, northern section)** From the parking area at Olifantsbos, cross the road and take the path up the hill. Keep left at intersections and you will arrive at Sirkelsvlei. To return by a different route, take the right-hand fork at the inland end of the vlei. You will soon see another fork, but there is a No Entry sign there, forcing you to continue right. This is a slightly longer route than the outward leg, but well worthwhile. There is also a path that takes you down to the coast, to join the Shipwreck Trail, but the flowers are not as prolific there as on the high path. |
| Entrance Gate parking area | **Route 8: Traverse over Rooihoogte to Sirkelsvlei (Central, northern section)** The path starts on the right once you have driven through the gate. This climbs up to skirt an unnamed bump, then drops slightly before climbing Rooihoogte – a great vantage point. Continue down to cross the road and carry on in a westerly direction before getting to Sirkelsvlei. From here you walk to Olifantsbos where you must leave a car. See the description above for alternative routes. |

Woody Ravine surveyed from the top, with Camps Bay below

# SAFETY ON THE MOUNTAIN

Mountain walks should always be regarded with caution and respect. Weather conditions can change quickly. Every year, people have to be rescued, and some die, because they set out badly prepared.

## Essential precautions

- Choose a well-marked route or one that you know well.
- Tell someone where you are going, how long your walk will be, your expected return time and let them know when you are back.
- Don't walk alone – for security reasons (muggings have occurred) and in case of an accident.
- Try not to take valuables with you.
- Carry plenty of water and some food.
- Always wear appropriate footwear.
- Apply sunscreen, even on cloudy days.
- Dress warmly. (It's often several degrees cooler at the top of a mountain.)
- Wear a hat, take a waterproof jacket and a warm top.
- Take a fully charged mobile phone with you. Save emergency contact numbers in your phone. (Be aware that certain areas on the mountain do not have mobile phone reception. Remember that text messages sometimes get through quicker than voice calls.)
- Take a whistle, small torch and basic first-aid kit.
- Stick to the footpaths; don't take short-cuts.
- When taking photographs, ensure that you have solid support and be careful of the ground underfoot. It is easy to slip on gravelly stones or wet rock.

## Crime

**If you are approached by muggers:**

- Keep calm.
- Do as they ask and hand over your belongings.
- Do not resist.
- Try to memorize their features for reporting to the police later

### USEFUL CONTACTS

(These details were correct at time of going to print.)

- **Cape Point Visitor Centre:** 021 780 9165
- **Metro Rescue:** Medical and Rescue Services  10177
  Rescue services and reporting crime  021 937 0300
  Cell phone emergency number (connects to Metro Rescue)  112
- **Mountain Rescue:** 021 948 9900
- **Permits from Table Mountain National Park offices:** 021 422 160
  Orange Kloof is a protected area so you need a permit to walk there. Booking well in advance is recommended. Hiking parties must be accompanied by a volunteer guide. Numbers are limited to parties of 6–12 people. Your permit will be emailed to you.
- **SANParks:** www.sanparks.org  021 780 9165
- **SA Weather Office:** www.weathersa.co.za (for an up-to-date weather forecast)
- **Table Mountain Cable Station:** www.tablemountain.net  021 424 8181
- **Table Mountain live weather forecast:** https://iweathar.co.za/stations.php (select Western Cape: 11 Table Mountain; 25 Cape Point)
- **Table Mountain National Park Emergency number (crime, rescue):** 086 110 6417

Jan–Dec · Up to 1m

## Wild Aster · Wilde-astertjie

*Felicia aethiopica*
Daisy family – Asteraceae

A leafy, spreading **shrub** with a hairy flower stem.
**Leaves:** Thin, lance-shaped, often bent slightly downwards.
**Flower head:** Single bright blue flower with yellow centre, borne on a long, leafless flower stem. Often found in mass displays.
**Distribution:** Fairly common.
**Habitat:** Upper and lower slopes, in bushy and rocky places.

June–Sept · Up to 1.2m

## Turquoise Bush Bugloss

*Lobostemon montanus*
Forget-me-not family – Boraginaceae

A large, erect, broad, sturdy, branching **shrub**.
**Leaves:** Silvery green, oval to oblong, hairy, stalkless. Leaves widen towards the tip.
**Flower head:** Blue or turquoise flowers, hairy outside, borne in a large **inflorescence** at the top of the **shrub**. Has thin 'feelers' (**stamens**) that stick out from the ends of the flowers.
**Distribution:** Fairly common.
**Habitat:** Lower sandstone slopes in bushy areas.

Aug–Jan · Up to 1m

## Blue Rocket Bugloss · Disselblaarluibos

*Lobostemon argenteus*
Forget-me-not family – Boraginaceae

A small, upright, bristly **shrublet**.
**Leaves:** Stalkless, silvery green, lance-shaped, partly hairy, with leaf edges curving under.
**Flower head:** Bright blue, funnel-shaped, with 5 'petals' and noticeably reddish **stamens**. Easily recognized by its upright **spike** from which flowers emerge at top and sides.
**Distribution:** Fairly common.
**Habitat:** Mainly drier, sandstone slopes.

## Little Blue Mouth
**Bloubekkie**

*Heliophila africana*
Mustard family – Brassicaceae

A rather stout, sparsely or densely hairy, sometimes sprawling, **annual herb.**
**Leaves:** Lance-shaped, sometimes **lobed**; the lower stalked, the upper stalkless.
**Flower head:** An exquisite blue or mauve flower with 4 rounded spreading petals, a white centre and bright yellow **stamen.**
**Distribution:** Common.
**Habitat:** Sandy soils among bushes and rocks.
**Notes:** Needs warm conditions before the flower will open. Closes again when it gets cold.

| Aug–Nov | Up to 40cm |
|---|---|

## Dark-eyed Bellflower

*Wahlenbergia capensis*
Bellflower family – Campanulaceae

A roughly hairy, erect **annual.**
**Leaves:** Stalkless, elliptical or paddle-shaped, wavy or toothed leaves, mainly towards the base of the stem.
**Flower head:** Solitary, bowl-shaped, pale blue flower with a darker hairy centre; borne on long stalks that are hairy at the base.
**Distribution:** Occasional, but when found, often in profusion.
**Habitat:** Sandstone slopes.

| Sept–Dec | Up to 50cm |
|---|---|

## White-eyed Roella

*Roella ciliata*
Bellflower family – Campanulaceae

An attractive flower with distinctive markings.
**Leaves:** Short, narrow, bristly, covering a thick stem.
**Flower head:** Single, cup-shaped flower with blue petals, dark inner ring, and white eye (at the base of the throat). Often found with others in clumps.
**Distribution:** Fairly common.
**Habitat:** Lower dry sandstone slopes.
**Notes:** *R. triflora* is similar, smaller, with a black eye at the base of the throat.

| Oct–Mar | Up to 50cm |
|---|---|

## Drip Disa
*Disa longicornu*
Orchid family – Orchidaceae

A seemingly frail, yet attractive, hanging **herb (geophyte)**.
**Leaves:** Basal, narrow, oval-pointed, pale green.
**Flower head:** Pale mauve, strikingly beautiful flower that grows in small groups. Each flower on an individual stem. Large hood, streaked by green veins.
**Distribution:** Rare – found only in a few locations and locally confined.
**Habitat:** Upper slopes, on damp to dripping, mossy, shady, south-facing rock faces.

Dec–Jan     Up to 20cm

## Early Blue Disa
*Disa purpurascens*
Orchid family – Orchidaceae

A slender, **tuberous perennial**.
**Leaves:** Erect, **basal**, dry, grass-like leaves **sheathing** the stem.
**Flower head:** An **inflorescence** of 1–7 sweetly scented flowers; each flower has a blue hood on top with side wings and a dark purple lip; yellow-green petals at the back of the hood.
**Distribution:** Occasionally found at Cape Point.
**Habitat:** Low, well-drained, sandy or stony areas.

Oct–Nov     Up to 60cm

## Babiana          Klein-bobbejaantjie
*Babiana villosula*
Iris family – Iridaceae

A dwarf **geophyte** with a deep-seated food store (**corm**).
**Leaves:** Hairy, lance-shaped, slender, floppy and longer than the flowering stem.
**Flower head:** Lightly scented, blue, mauve or violet flower with white centre. Petals are short, hairy, pleated and arranged fanwise.
**Distribution:** Fairly common.
**Habitat:** Mainly lower sandy slopes.

May–July     Up to 15cm

## Fringed Aristea
**Maagbossie**

*Aristea africana*
Iris family – Iridaceae

A small, evergreen **perennial**, often growing in clumps.
**Leaves:** Thin and narrow, pointed, somewhat sword-shaped.
**Flower head:** Low-growing, 6-petalled, bright blue,
short-lived flowers; 3 yellow **stamens** clearly visible. Each
flower lasts a day.
**Distribution:** Fairly common.
**Habitat:** Sandy slopes and plateaux.

Sept–Jan     Up to 15cm

## Blue Sceptre
**Blouvuurpyl**

*Aristea capitata*
Iris family – Iridaceae

A good-looking, tall, robust plant with a rounded stem
and short branches.
**Leaves:** Long, broad, **strap-like**, sword-shaped, evergreen.
**Flower head:** Dense **inflorescence** of blue saucer-shaped
flowers, crowded together and overlapping, that appear
on tall **spikes**.
**Distribution:** Common.
**Habitat:** Upper and lower slopes.

Oct–Nov     Up to 1.5m

## Agapanthus
**Bloulelie**

*Agapanthus africanus*
Agapanthus family – Agapanthaceae

An erect, long-stemmed evergreen **perennial**; flowers in
a large cluster, facing outwards.
**Leaves:** Long, leathery, **strap-shaped**, basal.
**Flower head:** Large, blue, funnel-shaped flowers, 12–30
in clusters at tip of main stem. A dark blue stripe runs
down the centre of each petal.
**Distribution:** Fairly common.
**Habitat:** Upper slopes, usually in rocky areas.
**Notes:** Flowers especially after fires.

Nov–Apr     Up to 70cm

Dec–Mar | Up to 50cm

## Black-eyed Roella
*Roella triflora*
Bellflower family – Campanulaceae

A scrambling or erect **shrublet**.
**Leaves:** Long and narrow, often in tufts; hairy, prickly-toothed on the leaf edges.
**Flower head:** Single, bell-like flowers – varying from pale blue to deep blue with dark blue-black centres – are borne at the end of a woody stem bristling with many pointed stiff leaves.
**Distribution:** Common in Silvermine, especially in Silvermine East.
**Habitat:** On sandy lower slopes mainly from Constantia Nek southwards.
**Notes:** Double flowers have been observed. Can grow in large clumps.

Sept–Dec | Up to 35cm

## Blue Satinflower                    Blousysie
*Geissorhiza aspera*
Iris family – Iridaceae

A tiny, neat, attractive flower with a wiry stem.
**Leaves:** Light green, long, thin, pointed, partly **sheathing** the flowering stem.
**Flower head:** Bright blue to violet (sometimes white) cup-like flowers with 6 glossy petals. Flowers grow as a string, all borne to one side, on short stalks towards stem tip.
**Distribution:** Common.
**Habitat:** Upper and lower slopes.

Aug–Nov | Up to 16cm

## Purple Clockflower              Kersblakertjie
*Moraea lugubris*
Iris family – Iridaceae

An erect **geophyte**.
**Leaves:** 2 dissimilar leaves: narrow lower leaf attached at ground level; shorter, broad-based upper leaf attached just beneath the flowers. The Afrikaans name refers to the **styles** which resemble little candlesticks.
**Flower head:** Bright blue flowers lasting one day.
**Distribution:** Rare, flowering after fire.
**Habitat:** Damp, sandy soils or seasonally wet sandstone in the southwest.

## Blue Pimpernel
**Blouselblommetjie**

*Anagallis arvensis*
Primrose family – Primulaceae

**A small, blue-flowered plant found individually or in small clumps.**
**Leaves:** Stalkless, well-veined, oval-pointed, spaced out on the flower stalk, in pairs, alternately opposite each other.
**Flower head:** Dark blue (more rarely, red) 5-petalled flower with red centre. Occurs usually at top of long flower stalk.
**Distribution:** Occasional.
**Habitat:** Lower slopes, moist areas, well-drained soils. Prefers shade.
**Notes:** Not indigenous, introduced from Europe. A red form occurs at Suikerbossie.

| Oct–Jan | Up to 40cm |

## Comb Flower
**Vleiblommetjie**

*Micranthus alopecuroides*
Iris family – Iridaceae

**An appealing, erect herb (geophyte) with a comb-like stem.**
**Leaves:** Long, flat, thin, pointed, with an easily seen mid-vein.
**Flower head:** Tiny pale to dark blue flowers tipped with red, closely packed together; occur in 2 rows up the stem.
**Distribution:** Rare – found only in a few locations.
**Habitat:** Sandy places.

| Oct–Jan | Up to 45cm |

## Wild Lobelia
**Kussinglobelia**

*Lobelia coronopifolia*
Lobelia family – Lobeliaceae

**A tufted, erect perennial with a long, bare stem.**
**Leaves:** Basal, tufted, dark green, stalkless, deeply lobed; usually hairy.
**Flower head:** Long-tubed, hairless, usually purple or dark blue flowers grow at the end of long, wiry, leafless stems. 5 petals: 3 broader, widening at the front, and 2 smaller ones standing up like small horns. White anthers are clearly visible.
**Distribution:** Common.
**Habitat:** Dry sandy to stony lower slopes.
**Notes:** Occasionally pink *L. coronopifolia* flowers are found on Table Mountain and in Silvermine.

| Nov–Mar | Up to 40cm |

Nov–Mar | Up to 40cm

## Wiry Lobelia

*Lobelia setacea*
Lobelia family – Lobeliaceae

A tufted, erect or sprawling **perennial** with slender stems, sparsely branched.
**Leaves:** Stalkless, narrow and thin; scant leaves scattered along the stem.
**Flower head:** Hairless, blue- to violet-petalled flowers with centre of the lowest petals showing white. Flowers are loosely spread at the top of green flower stalks.
**Distribution:** Frequent.
**Habitat:** Damp sand flats and low slopes.

Jan–Dec | Up to 50cm

## Pine-leaved Lobelia

*Lobelia pinifolia*
Lobelia family – Lobeliaceae

A semi-erect **shrublet** with leaves that run up the stem to the flower head.
**Leaves:** Closely packed, overlapping, pine-like.
**Flower head:** Blue or purple flowers with 5 petals, 3 larger ones below, 2 small above, with 2 sets of white-haired **anthers** clearly seen (like mini 'tusks').
**Distribution:** Frequently found.
**Habitat:** Among rocks and bushes, often bordering on footpaths.
**Notes:** The flower head of *L. coronopifolia* is somewhat similar, but that flower has a long, bare stem.

Oct–Jan | Up to 4m

## Blue Pea, Fountain Bush     Bloukeurtjie

*Psoralea aphylla*
Pea family – Fabaceae

An erect, willowy **shrub** or tree with broom-like branches that tend to hang pendulously when in flower.
**Leaves:** Almost leafless – tiny, narrow, ascending, egg-shaped to lance-shaped leaves occur only on young branches.
**Flower head:** Single mauve to deep-blue-and-white pea-type flowers, consisting of a broad joined petal with 2 smaller lips of a paler colour, are borne at the end of branches on long, drooping stems.
**Distribution:** Occasional.
**Habitat:** In marshy places, alongside streams.

## Blue Disa
**Bloumoederkappie**

*Disa graminifolia*
Orchid family – Orchidaceae

A beautiful, slender-stemmed, erect, **tuberous perennial**.
**Leaves:** Narrow, grass-like, **basal**; they wither and go brown at time of flowering.
**Flower head:** Attractive, sweet-scented, violet-purple flower, with large upper hood, 2 side petals and, at front, 'Ouma's tongue'. Within the hood, inner petals are tipped with green.
**Distribution:** Fairly common.
**Habitat:** Upper slopes, peaks and summits, among **fynbos** and reeds in dry sunny areas.

| Feb–Apr | Up to 60cm |
|---|---|

## Common Babiana
**Bobbejaantjie**

*Babiana ambigua*
Iris family – Iridaceae

A small, short-stemmed dwarf **geophyte**.
**Leaves:** Narrow, ribbed, hairy, oblong to lance-shaped, longer than the flower.
**Flower head:** Blue (pink, mauve), fragrant, 6-petalled flower with white to cream markings. Flowers vary in size and colour.
**Distribution:** Occasional.
**Habitat:** Sandy soil, lower slopes.

| Aug–Sept | Up to 8cm |
|---|---|

## Otholobium
**Skaapbostee**

*Otholobium fruticans*
Pea family – Fabaceae

An attractive, well-branched, bushy **shrublet**.
**Leaves:** Narrow, oval-shaped, with hairy edges, tips turned down, tightly clustered in 3s.
**Flower head:** Consists of a lovely combination of many small mauve-and-white flowers, interspersed with green **bracts**, in a rounded head. Flowers seem to cascade downwards, almost like a tiered wedding cake.
**Distribution:** Rare – found only in a few locations on Table Mountain and occasionally in Silvermine.
**Habitat:** Lower slopes, sandy soils.

| Sept–Dec | Up to 1m |
|---|---|

Sep–Nov | Up to 15cm

## Painted Cabong

**Koringblommetjie**

*Codonorhiza corymbosa*
Iris family – Iridaceae

A short, **cormous geophyte**.
**Leaves:** A single **basal** leaf, longer than the stem, with a few smaller leaves on the stem.
**Flower head:** Many stalkless flowers, light to dark purple-blue with a central white star, borne in large clusters on a much-branched flowering stalk.
**Distribution:** Locally common on granite slopes on Signal Hill; occasional elsewhere.
**Habitat:** Sandy and granitic flats and lower slopes.

Aug–Nov | Up to 2m

## Bush Blue Pea

*Psoralea aculeata*
Pea family – Fabaceae

An erect, densely branched and leafy aromatic **shrub**.
**Leaves:** Many, small, semi-folded, closely packed (in 3s), with prickly hook-pointed tips.
**Flower head:** Violet pea-type flowers, scattered along the upper end of branches, provide a mass display. Each solitary flower on individual tiny branchlet.
**Distribution:** Fairly common.
**Habitat:** Upper slopes, often near water.

Aug–Feb | Up to 3m

## Fountain Bush

**Fonteinbos**

*Psoralea pinnata*
Pea family – Fabaceae

An erect **shrub**, or small willowy tree, with a fairly barren stem.
**Leaves:** Ascending, thin and rounded, pine-like.
**Flower head:** Sweet-scented, lilac-blue and white pea-type flowers emerge, in mass display, between leaves towards tips of branches.
**Distribution:** Frequently found.
**Habitat:** Upper mountain slopes, damp areas, near dams, streams or forest margins.

## Purple Powderpuff

**Blouaarbossie**

*Pseudoselago serrata*
Sutera family – Scrophulariaceae

**A handsome, erect, leafy shrublet with a stout stem.**
**Leaves:** Oblong, overlapping, leathery, pointed tips
bending backwards, edges slightly toothed with a
reddish tinge.
**Flower head:** Tiny, mauve, **tubular** flowers, densely
packed at the top of the plant in a flat-topped or
slightly rounded cluster. The mauve-orange patches are
unopened buds.
**Distribution:** Frequently found.
**Habitat:** Mainly upper mountain slopes.

| Oct–Mar | Up to 90cm |
|---|---|

## Wild Sage

**Bloublomsalie**

*Salvia africana-caerulea*
Mint family – Lamiaceae

**The first blue sage to flower. The flower shape resembles
a parrot's beak.**
**Leaves:** At base, small, opposite, toothed, grey-white
underneath. Upper leaves are bigger.
**Flower head:** Pale blue to mauve, hairy flower. Upper
petal hooded, lower petal has a white patch with blue
spots. Leaves and flowers are spaced up the stem.
**Distribution:** Common.
**Habitat:** Upper and lower slopes.
**Notes:** *S. chamelaeagnea* looks somewhat similar.

| Sept–Jan | Up to 2m |
|---|---|

## Sea Lavender

**Brakbossie**

*Limonium scabrum*
Plumbago family – Plumbaginaceae

**A tufted dwarf perennial, densely branched.**
**Leaves:** Paddle-shaped leaves form a **rosette** at the base of
the plant, where they usually wither by flowering time.
**Flower head:** Numerous pale mauve papery flowers
occur at the top of intricately branched stems. The lower
branchlets are often sterile.
**Distribution:** Frequent.
**Habitat:** Sandy soil near the sea.

| Dec–Feb | Up to 30cm |
|---|---|

## Lilac Powderpuff

*Pseudoselago spuria*
Sutera family – Scrophulariaceae

**An attractive, erect shrub with many branched flowering stems.**
**Leaves:** Thin, ascending, lance-shaped, toothed; taper in size going up the stem.
**Flower head:** Tiny mauve flowers occur at the top of thin, strong stems, in a densely packed, flat-topped cluster. The mauve-orange patches are unopened buds.
**Distribution:** Common.
**Habitat:** Common amid rocks on mountain slopes.

Oct–Jan | Up to 75cm

## Table Mountain Plume Aster
### Pluimastertjie

*Zyrphelis taxifolia*
Daisy family – Asteraceae

**A slender, sprawling, sparsely hairy shrublet.**
**Leaves:** Small, needle-like, minutely toothed.
**Flower head:** Solitary, blue to mauve petals with a yellow centre, at the top of a long flower stem.
**Distribution:** Common.
**Habitat:** Damp sandstone slopes.

Sept–Feb | Up to 40cm

## Smooth-leaved Bush Bugloss

*Lobostemon glaucophyllus*
Forget-me-not family – Boraginaceae

**A common, large, erect and branching shrub.**
**Leaves:** Grey-green, almost entirely smooth, stalkless, lance-shaped leaves that vary in size.
**Flower head:** Pink or blue flowers, funnel-shaped and hairless outside, in short clusters at the branch tips.
**Distribution:** Common.
**Habitat:** Mainly western side, sandy slopes.

July–Oct | Up to 1.2m

## Fleur-de-lys

**Blou-uintjie**

*Moraea tripetala*
Iris family – Iridaceae

A small, eye-catching flower of varying colour.
**Leaves:** Single, **basal**, narrow, longer than flower.
**Flower head:** Unmistakable, blue or purple-violet flower,
with 3 propeller-like petals, each with small white or
yellow triangle; occurs singly on an erect flower stalk.
**Distribution:** Common.
**Habitat:** Upper and lower mountain slopes and flat areas.

Aug–Jan     Up to 45cm

## Nightshade

**Slangappelbos**

*Solanum tomentosum*
Potato family – Solanaceae

A straggling, prickly **shrub**. The golden-brown stems have
**1.2cm spines, usually straight, sometimes recurving.**
**Leaves:** Green, egg-shaped to rounded, densely felted
underneath; curling slightly inwards, wavy at the edges.
**Flower head:** 5-petalled, star-shaped, mauve, purple or
violet flowers are found in small clusters at the top of
the flower stalks. White flowers occasionally seen. The
plant has bright orange spherical berries initially, which
become nearly red when ripe.
**Distribution:** Frequent.
**Habitat:** In dry bushy places, particularly at the foot of cliffs.

Jul–Oct     Up to 1m

## Blue Pea Bush

**Blouertjiebos**

*Amphithalea imbricata*
Pea family – Fabaceae

A handsome, tall, erect **shrub** with spreading branches.
**Leaves:** Soft, shiny, grey-green, distinctly veined, oval
to lance-shaped; arranged in overlapping, alternately
opposite pairs.
**Flower head:** Mass of small mauve to purple-violet flowers
that are nestled among leaves towards end of branches.
**Distribution:** Rare – found only in a few locations.
**Habitat:** Kloofs, upper slopes, also damp stream banks.

Dec–June     Up to 1.8m

Sep–Jan | Up to 40cm

## Dainty Butterfly Bush
*Polygala garcinii*
Polygala family – Polygalaceae

A small, weak-stemmed, frail-looking **shrub**, woody at the base.
**Leaves:** Thin, narrow, needle-like.
**Flower head:** Small flowers, occurring up the stem – a pink 'bird' with tufted white face and rounded side petals.
**Distribution:** Common.
**Habitat:** Upper and lower slopes.

Aug–Oct | Up to 2m

## September Butterfly Bush
**Blouertjieboom**

*Polygala myrtifolia*
Polygala family – Polygalaceae

A large, sprawling, evergreen, leafy and prolifically flowering **shrub**.
**Leaves:** Variable in shape, some flat and oval, others narrower with edges rolled under.
**Flower head:** Purple-pink and white flowers, in an elongated display towards branch tips. Oval-shaped petals are whitish-pink underneath.
**Distribution:** Occasional.
**Habitat:** Rocky slopes, especially in forest areas and near streams.

Jan–Dec | Up to 2m

## Spiny Purple Gorse
**Kastybos**
*Muraltia heisteria*
Polygala family – Polygalaceae

A loosely upright, prickly **shrub** with spreading branches.
**Leaves:** Small, prickly, spine-tipped.
**Flower head:** Small purple flowers with white side petals, scattered between leaves towards branch tips.
**Distribution:** Frequently found.
**Habitat:** Widespread, but mainly on lower slopes.

## Polygala
### *Polygala bracteolata*
Polygala family – Polygalaceae

**A thinly branched, spreading shrub.**
**Leaves:** Narrow, lance-shaped, on long flower stalks.
**Flower head:** Pea-type, purple-pink and white flower with 2 pink wings and a white crested fringe; occurs on long pink flower stalks in crowded clusters towards top ends of branches.
**Distribution:** Frequently found.
**Habitat:** Upper and lower slopes.

| Jul–Dec | Up to 1m |
| --- | --- |

## Granny Bonnet                    Moederkappie
### *Disperis capensis*
Orchid family – Orchidaceae

**A small, erect orchid (geophyte).**
**Leaves:** 1 or 2; long, narrow, pointed, **basal**; also has a few small pointed leaves that **sheathe** the stem.
**Flower head:** Solitary, dark pink-red flower with a well-defined hood and 'horns' at the top of a short, slender stem. Shape of flower head from the front looks like a woman's bonnet.
**Distribution:** Occasional.
**Habitat:** Upper and lower dampish mountain slopes among thick **fynbos**.
**Notes:** Pollinated by carpenter bees.

| Jun–Aug | Up to 35cm |
| --- | --- |

## Indigofera
### *Indigofera filifolia*
Pea family – Fabaceae

**A tall, erect, branching shrub.**
**Leaves:** Long, thin, thread-like. Almost leafless except for very young plants.
**Flower head:** Bright pinkish-mauve, pea-like flowers, each with an upright, half-round petal above and 2 small petals below; appear towards the tops of tall, straw-thin, green branchlets.
**Distribution:** Rare – found only in a few locations.
**Habitat:** Seen near streams in sheltered areas on southern slopes.

| Feb–Apr | Up to 2m |
| --- | --- |

Dec–May     Up to 60cm

## Purple Senecio

*Senecio purpureus*
Daisy family – Asteraceae

A **perennial** hairy **herb** with thistle-like flower head.
**Leaves:** Large, widely spaced, deeply **lobed**, found up the stem.
**Flower head:** Purple flower, with no petals, occurs on a short stalk at top of a long, dark pink flower stem.
**Distribution:** Occasional.
**Habitat:** Upper and lower slopes.

Nov–Jan     Up to 25cm

## Summer Pipes

*Thereianthus bracteolatus*
Iris family – Iridaceae

A rigid, unbranched, **cormous geophyte** with zigzagging stems.
**Leaves:** Rounded, long, **basal, sheathing** the stem, less so higher up where they taper to a point.
**Flower head:** Up to 12 flowers emerge up the stem, crowded together, supported by brown **bracts**. The flowers have 6 petals, variable, purple to violet to blue, with protruding **styles**.
**Distribution:** Occasional.
**Habitat:** Sandy soil and on mountain slopes and plateaux.

Nov–Dec     Up to 50cm

## Wild Pink            Wilde-angelier

*Dianthus albens*
Carnation family – Caryophyllaceae

A hairless **perennial**.
**Leaves:** Narrow, grass-like leaves, opposite, leaf edges roughish.
**Flower head:** 1 or a few flowers, petals white at centre becoming pink to purple towards the irregularly notched edges.
**Distribution:** Occasional.
**Habitat:** Sandy flats and slopes, often coastal, more frequent in the south.

## Cape Scabious
Koringblom

*Scabiosa africana*
Scabious family – Dipsacaceae

A lovely, tall, branched **perennial**.
**Leaves:** Large, **basal**, roughly oval-pointed with irregularly toothed edges and prominent mid-vein.
**Flower head:** Mauve, half-round, disc-shaped flower head consisting of tiny, densely packed flowers. Single flower on each long flower stalk.
**Distribution:** Common.
**Habitat:** Mainly eastern slopes in sheltered, bushy areas.
**Notes:** A lookalike, *S. columbaria*, also appears on the mountain but is white.

| Aug–Mar | Up to 1m |
|---|---|

## Tortoise Berry
Skilpadbessie

*Muraltia spinosa*
Polygala family – Polygalaceae

A much-branched, hard, thorny **shrub** with many lengthy, green, stiff, spine-tipped stems.
**Leaves:** Small, green, short-stalked oblong leaves occur sparsely up light green stems.
**Flower head:** Small white and pink flowers, somewhat pea-like in appearance, found up and down the branches of this widely spreading **shrub**. The flowers bear small, rounded, edible fruit which turn yellow and later red. Ostriches and tortoises eat this fruit, hence the common name.
**Distribution:** Frequent.
**Habitat:** Sandy flats and lower slopes.

| Jun–Jul | Up to 1m |
|---|---|

## Needle Ragwort

*Senecio umbellatus*
Daisy family – Asteraceae

An erect, finely leaved **perennial**, stems sparsely hairy near the base.
**Leaves:** Narrow, alternate, slightly toothed, divided leaves, longer at the base, with leaf edges turned down.
**Flower head:** Mauve or purple radiate petals (rarely white) with yellow centres, in loosely branched clusters surrounded by a series of narrow **bracts**.
**Distribution:** Occasional, but sometimes prolific.
**Habitat:** Moist lower sandstone slopes.

| Oct–Dec | Up to 80cm |
|---|---|

## Lady's Hand
**Blouraaptol**

*Cyanella hyacinthoides*
Cyanella family – Tecophilaeaceae

**A small, annual geophyte.**
**Leaves:** Large, broad, long, pointed, rising from the base.
**Flower head:** Slightly scented, pale blue (pink or white) flowers, with 6 backward-turned petals; appear alternately from slender stalks, up an erect stem.
**Distribution:** Fairly common.
**Habitat:** Mainly on lower, drier slopes.
**Notes:** The yellow **stamens** represent a lady's hand complete with fingernails.

SM
Oct–Jan | Up to 50cm

## Bloodroot
**Rooiwortel**

*Dilatris corymbosa*
Bloodroot family – Haemodoraceae

**An unmistakable, erect, perennial herb (geophyte).**
**Leaves:** Stiff, long, narrow, sword-shaped, arising from the base of the plant.
**Flower head:** Large, mauve, densely packed, flat-topped **inflorescence** consisting of tiny, hairy flowers with 6 pointed petals with red-brown tips. Flower head grows on a hairless, grey stem.
**Distribution:** Rare – found only in a few locations.
**Habitat:** Mountain slopes, fairly common in Orange Kloof and occasional in Silvermine.
**Notes:** *D. pillansii* is similar but has shortish **stamens** nestled within the petals; *D. corymbosa* has longer **stamens** that rise just above the petals.

CM

Oct–Jan | Up to 60cm

## Bush Felicia
**Bosastertjie**

*Felicia fruticosa*
Daisy family – Asteraceae

**A rounded, densely branched, bushy shrub.**
**Leaves:** Small, narrow, pointed; sprout from the stem in small tufts. Have slight gland spots.
**Flower head:** Each flower, borne singly, has blue to mauve petals with a yellow centre. Grows on an almost leafless flower stalk. Masses of flowers can appear on a large bush.
**Distribution:** Frequently found.
**Habitat:** Upper and lower slopes in drier areas.

GN
Sep–Jan | Up to 1m

## Common Romulea — Rooiknikkertjie
*Romulea rosea*
Iris family – Iridaceae

**A small, low-growing perennial geophyte, variably coloured.**
**Leaves:** Long, thin, stiff, grass-like with 4 small grooves, much taller than the flower.
**Flower head:** Light pink to lilac-pink, 6-petalled flower with a pale yellow cup (throat), which is often darkly streaked.
**Distribution:** Common.
**Habitat:** Lower slopes, especially more sandy or gravelly areas.

Jul–Oct | Up to 40cm

## Everlasting Vygie — Altydvygie
*Erepsia anceps*
Ice Plant family – Aizoaceae

**An erect, woody, lightly branched perennial.**
**Leaves:** Narrow, curving backwards at the tip, spaced up the stem, in pairs opposite each other.
**Flower head:** Multi-petalled, pink or magenta, daisy-like flowers with a yellow centre; occur at the end of branches.
**Distribution:** Frequently found.
**Habitat:** Widespread. Upper and lower rocky slopes.
**Notes:** Petals tend to remain open in overcast weather.

Dec–Apr | Up to 30cm

## Rough Swordweed — Heuningbos
*Corymbium africanum*
Daisy family – Asteraceae

**A tufted perennial with a thin, tough stem.**
**Leaves:** **Basal,** long, thin, narrow, **strap-like,** parallel-veined. Up the stem: small, widely spaced, lance-shaped.
**Flower head:** Tiny pink (purple or white) flower heads form dense, flat or slightly rounded clusters at tip of the flower stalks.
**Distribution:** Fairly common.
**Habitat:** Sandy slopes.
**Notes:** Flowers especially well after fires.

Oct–Jan | Up to 30cm

Jun–Nov     Up to 5m

## Tree Sweet Pea     Keurtjie
*Podalyria calyptrata*
Pea family – Fabaceae

Large branching **shrub** or small tree, with prolific mauve-pink flowers.
**Leaves:** Large, green-grey, **simple**, oval-pointed, with easily seen veins.
**Flower head:** Large, showy, mauve-pink, pea-type, sweetly scented, 5-petalled flowers crowd the branch tips. Back petal is especially large, rounded and deeply notched, going white towards its base.
**Distribution:** Fairly common.
**Habitat:** Mainly lower slopes, often in ravines/damp areas.

Aug–Feb     Up to 1.2m

## Glossy Lilac Berry     Stinkbos
*Teedia lucida*
Sutera family – Scrophulariaceae

A hairless, sprawling **shrublet**.
**Leaves:** Large, glossy, finely toothed, wide-spreading oval leaves, opposite each other on long flower stalks.
**Flower head:** Purple or mauve flowers, petals deeply **lobed**, found in small clusters at the top of branch stems. The plant has drab purple or yellowish-brown berries (green when unripe).
**Distribution:** Uncommon.
**Habitat:** Grows in rocky crevices and cracks.

Jan–Dec     Up to 1m

## Hairy-flower Heath
*Erica hirtiflora*
Erica family – Ericaceae

An erect, bushy, branching **shrub**.
**Leaves:** Small, ascending, needle-like, crowded, in tufts of 4.
**Flower head:** Small, mauve-pink, oval, covered with short, soft hairs. Often found in mass display on the mountainside.
**Distribution:** Common.
**Habitat:** Particularly common in high-rainfall, damp or marshy areas.
**Notes:** One of the most common ericas, often covering mountainsides in season.

## Cape Anemone — Syblom

*Anemone tenuifolia*
Ranunculus family – Ranunculaceae

A sturdy, tufted **perennial** with feathery petals.
**Leaves:** Basal, dark green, toothed, divided into many segments.
**Flower head:** Pinkish-white silky petals and bright yellow to brown centre; petal undersides are darker pink. Single flower borne on a long, pinkish velvety stem.
**Distribution:** Fairly common.
**Habitat:** Upper slopes, mainly on eastern side in good rainfall areas.

| Jun–Nov | Up to 60cm |

## Mountain Carnation — Bergangelier

*Lachnaea densiflora*
Daphne family – Thymelaeaceae

A slender, sparsely branched **shrublet** with stems reddish when young.
**Leaves:** Long, narrowly rounded, spine-tipped.
**Flower head:** Densely packed, cream to pink-coloured, in well-defined rounded heads.
**Distribution:** Locally common in Cape Point.
**Habitat:** Mainly coastal sandy flats and lower slopes.

| Aug–Dec | Up to 50cm |

## Flats Satinflower

*Geissorhiza tenella*
Iris family – Iridaceae

A small **perennial** with long, sticky stems.
**Leaves:** 3 sticky leaves, long and narrow, edges raised, surrounding the stem; the lower 1 is longer, the upper 2 are shorter.
**Flower head:** 1–6 thin, propeller-shaped flowers, cream above, pink below, with prominent orange **stamens**, flowering at the top of **spikes. Bracts** green.
**Distribution:** Occasional.
**Habitat:** Seasonally wet flats and dunes.

| Oct–Nov | Up to 35cm |

## Porcelain Satin Flower    Pienk Satynblom

*Geissorhiza ovata*
Iris family – Iridaceae

A small **perennial** with sparsely branched or unbranched flowering stems.
**Leaves:** 2 broad, oval, leathery leaves, rounded at the tip, spread almost flat on the ground.
**Flower head:** Moderately large flowers, white to pale pink on top, pink underneath. They grow 2–4 per **spike**, positioned spirally, with green **bracts** below, sometimes flushed with pink.
**Distribution:** Common, often appears after a fire.
**Habitat:** Sandstone slopes and flats in the south.

Aug–Oct            Up to 15cm

## Fountain Heath

*Erica fontana*
Erica family – Ericaceae

An erect, densely leafy, upright **shrub**.
**Leaves:** Small, thin, needle-like and hairy, slightly curved, ascending, on brownish to red stems.
**Flower head:** Medium-sized, tubular, white or pinkish-white flowers facing outwards in clusters ascending the leaf stems.
**Distribution:** Rare, found only at Cape Point.
**Habitat:** Wetlands and adjacent seepage areas.

Oct–May            Up to 1.8m

## Painted Lady            Bergpypie

*Gladiolus carneus*
Iris family – Iridaceae

An erect, **perennial herb**. The best-known gladiolus on the mountain.
**Leaves:** Long, thin, partially **sheathing** the stem. Single **basal** leaf appears after flowering.
**Flower head:** Pink or white touched with pink, with a pale pink, funnel-shaped throat. Lower petals have variable red markings on the inside; like an inverted wine glass.
**Distribution:** Fairly common.
**Habitat:** Upper slopes, mainly eastern side, sheltered areas.
**Notes:** Especially noticeable after fires.

Aug–Dec            Up to 60cm

## Hairy-leaved Buchu       Bergboegoe
*Agathosma ciliaris*
Citrus family – Rutaceae

**A small, bushy, evergreen shrublet with heath-like foliage.**
**Leaves:** Short, oval, pointed, hairy (hairless with age), aniseed scented.
**Flower head:** Tiny white or mauve flowers on reddish flower stalks; flowers appear in densely packed, rounded, terminal clusters.
**Distribution:** Common.
**Habitat:** Mainly upper slopes.
**Notes:** *A. ciliata* is similar but less common. Whiter, bigger, with larger, hairy, lance-shaped leaves.

Jun–Nov       Up to 45cm

## Peninsula Silky Puff
*Diastella divaricata*
Protea family – Proteaceae

**A low, single-stemmed, sprawling shrublet often found in dense stands.**
**Leaves:** Flat, egg-shaped to oblong, round-tipped.
**Flower head:** Broad, pink flowers with a very short floral tube appear mainly at the ends of branches.
**Distribution:** Fairly common.
**Habitat:** Found on Silvermine's sandy plateau and sandstone slopes, especially in the south.
**Notes:** This is the smallest protea.

Jan–Dec       Up to 50cm

## Pink Everlasting       Pienksewejaartjie
*Syncarpha canescens*
Daisy family – Asteraceae

**A sparsely-branched, closely leafy shrublet.**
**Leaves:** Small, stalkless, overlapping, grey-felted, oblong leaves with rounded tips which press close to the stem.
**Flower head:** Pink flowers, darker at the centre, solitary at the branch tips, surrounded by several series of pointed papery **bracts** that are pink to red.
**Distribution:** Frequent.
**Habitat:** On rocky sandstone slopes and flats

Nov–Jul       Up to 30cm

Jan–Mar — Up to 50cm

## Autumn Pipes — Herfspypie

*Gladiolus brevifolius*
Iris family – Iridaceae

A delicate, erect, sometimes scented, **cormous geophyte**.
**Leaves:** Few, short, **sheathing** the stem, the lowest rust-tipped. Single **basal** leaf appears after flowering.
**Flower head:** Frail-looking pale pink flower, with 3 upright petals above and 3 narrower ones with yellow spade-like markings below. Often several flowers on stem.
**Distribution:** Rare on Table Mountain but common further south.
**Habitat:** Upper slopes, mainly in the south.
**Notes:** *G. monticola* similar, more apricot in colour, with a more open, bell-like face.

Sep–Dec — Up to 2m

## Wild Mallow — Kussandroos

*Anisodontea scabrosa*
Hibiscus family – Malvaceae

An erect, indigenous, evergreen, coarse-textured, leafy, aromatic **shrub**.
**Leaves:** Rough-textured, somewhat crumpled, sticky, hairy, veined, with deeply cut edges.
**Flower head:** Fragile, square-looking pink flowers with 5 broad petals, yellow centres and red markings; occur singly, towards branch tips.
**Distribution:** Rare – found only in a few locations.
**Habitat:** Lower slopes, sheltered bushy areas on sandy soils. Not found in Silvermine.
**Notes:** A common garden plant.

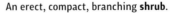

Sep–Jan — Up to 60cm

## Grand Stringbark

*Lachnaea grandiflora*
Daphne family – Thymelaeaceae

An erect, compact, branching **shrub**.
**Leaves:** Thick, pointed, oblong to elliptical leaves – opposite, in 4 rows, densely overlapping – grow up the stem, pressed against it.
**Flower head:** Large, 4-petalled, pink or white flowers, silky outside with pointed hairs, are borne singly at the ends of branchlets.
**Distribution:** Fairly common, confined to a limited area.
**Habitat:** Mainly found in the south.
**Notes:** Some shrubs grow as high as a metre.

## Wingfig

*Cleretum herrei*
Ice Plant family – Aizoaceae

A water-retaining, ground-spreading, **annual herb** adapted to arid climates and soil.
**Leaves:** Green, flat and fleshy, covered with glistening water cells, red around the lyre-shaped, irregular edges. Re-sprouting after fires.
**Flower head:** Solitary pink, can be tinged with white, with a yellow-green centre.
**Distribution:** Occasional, frequent after fires.
**Habitat:** Sandy soil on disturbed ground.

| Jul–Oct | Up to 15cm |

## Strawberry Snakebush  Knoppieslangbos

*Stoebe rosea*
Daisy family – Asteraceae

A stiff, much-branched, densely leaved **shrublet.**
**Leaves:** Tiny needle-like sharp-tipped leaves; crowded, twisting, with rolled-up leaf edges, grow closely up the stem.
**Flower head:** Each flower head is spherical, clusters of pink **florets** emerging through white, feathery pappus bristles at the top of flower **spikes.**
**Distribution:** Occasional.
**Habitat:** Sandstone slopes on eastern side of Silvermine and further south. Usually found in high, rocky areas catching the Southeaster cloud.
**Notes:** Endemic to the southern Peninsula.

| Jan–Mar | Up to 50cm |

## Little Snow  Kapokkie

*Erica bruniades*
Erica family – Ericaceae

A loose or compact bushy **shrublet.**
**Leaves:** Long and narrow with blunt tips and fine white hairs, on a brown-pink stem.
**Flower head:** Tiny pink, urn-shaped flowers, nodding, in concentrated clusters at the end of stems, flowers covered with a mass of short, soft, white woolly hairs (the 'snow'), dark pink **anthers** just protruding from the flower mouth.
**Distribution:** Common.
**Habitat:** Damp, peaty flats.

| Jul–Jan | Up to 50cm |

Apr–Sep | Up to 80cm

## Candlestick

*Stilbe ericoides*
Stilbe family – Stilbaceae

An erect, multi-stemmed **shrublet** with velvety stems.
**Leaves:** Small, long and narrow, in **whorls** of 3 to 4 up the stem.
**Flower head:** A mass of pink flowers crowded into a spherical **spike**, surrounded by far-reaching **stamens** which give this plant a shining bottlebrush look.
**Distribution:** Occasional. Re-sprouting after fire.
**Habitat:** Dry sandy flats and limestone hills in the coastal south.

Aug–Oct | Up to 30cm

## Ruschia

*Ruschia sarmentosa*
Ice Plant family – Aizoaceae

A sprawling **perennial**, with a habit of rooting wherever the stem nodes are in contact with the soil.
**Leaves:** Green, smooth, thick, fleshy, sharply keeled, loosely spread, pointing, up to 8cm long with a small leaf tip.
**Flower head:** 3–9 lookalike flowers, petals rose to mauve, white centre, with rounded **stamens**, providing a colourful **inflorescence** at the top of stalk stems.
**Distribution:** Occasional.
**Habitat:** Sandy areas of Cape Point.

Oct–Apr | Up to 40cm

## Stonecrop

*Crassula pellucida*
Crassula family – Crassulaceae

A soft, **succulent**, scrambling **perennial**.
**Leaves:** Small, oval-pointed, in pairs opposite each other; faintly toothed; grow directly from round reddish stem.
**Flower head:** Small, star-shaped, rose-pink flower with 5 pointed petals that become white in the centre. Several flower clusters grow towards the top of leafy stems.
**Distribution:** Occasional.
**Habitat:** Upper slopes in damp areas, such as ravines.

## Wild Cineraria
**Strandblommetjie**

*Senecio elegans*
Daisy family – Asteraceae

An **annual herb**, densely covered with gland-tipped hairs.
**Leaves:** Variably sized, fleshy, deeply **lobed** or divided leaves, often clammy to the touch.
**Flower head:** Flowers with purple-pink petals and a yellow centre grow at the top of widely separated stems to form a loosely branched **inflorescence**.
**Distribution:** Common.
**Habitat:** Lower mountain slopes.
**Notes:** The leaves of *S. elegans* can be cooked and eaten like spinach. The plant becomes very **succulent** when near the sea.

Jul–Mar | Up to 1m

## River Indigo

*Indigofera cytisoides*
Pea family – Fabaceae

An erect, robust **shrub**, single-stemmed, branches hairy.
**Leaves:** Stalkless to short stalks; 3–5 green-grey leaflets on each side of the stalk, minutely haired, inversely lance-shaped with pointed tips.
**Flower head:** Pink to purple flowers in profusion at the top of an unbranched, elongated **inflorescence**, maturing from the bottom upwards on robust flower stalks.
**Distribution:** Frequent, but rare in the south.
**Habitat:** Near rivers and on mountainsides.

Mar–May | Up to 3m

## Livingstone Daisy
**Bokbaaivygie**

*Cleretum bellidiforme*
Ice Plant family – Aizoaceae

A dwarf, compact **succulent**, Winter-growing yet sun-loving, forms a low ground cover with spreading branches.
**Leaves:** Green with maroon tints, narrow, tongue-like to paddle-shaped, covered with bladder-like water storage cells that glisten in bright sunlight.
**Flower head:** Solitary but numerous brightly coloured flowers grow at the top of fleshy stalks; narrow petals with purple or yellow **stamens**. Petals appear in a variety of colours: magenta, pink, salmon, orange, yellow or nearly white. The flower opens widely in bright sunlight.
**Distribution:** Widely distributed.
**Habitat:** Commonly seen on open, sandy flats, also favours gravelly clay slopes.

Aug–Oct | Up to 25mm

## Purple Sour Fig

**Elandsvy**

*Carpobrotus acinaciformis*
Ice Plant family – Aizoaceae

A **perennial** with fast-growing, trailing stems, spreading rapidly at ground level.
**Leaves:** Grass-green, sabre-shaped leaves, densely packed and matted together enabling rapid growth; fire-resistant and drought-tolerant.
**Flower head:** Large, solitary, magenta-purple, daisy-like flowers grow at the end of a short stalk.
**Distribution:** Common.
**Habitat:** Coastal sand in the south.

Jun–Jan     Up to 9cm

## Hairy Pea

*Indigofera glomerata*
Pea family – Fabaceae

A prostrate, densely leafy **shrublet**, woody with many branches, spreading.
**Leaves:** Densely overlapping, egg-shaped to oval leaves, split in 3s, softly white-hairy, tips curved and pointed.
**Flower head:** Small pinkish-purple flowers on short stalks, petals hairy, nestling in the leaves.
**Distribution:** Frequent.
**Habitat:** Dry slopes, lowlands and mountain **fynbos**.

Aug–Nov     Up to 30cm

## Iron Heath

*Erica ferrea*
Erica family – Ericaceae

An erect, sparse, compact sticky **shrub**.
**Leaves:** Leaves in **whorls** of 3–4, elliptical, toothed.
**Flower head:** Pink to magenta flowers, small, broadly urn-shaped, found in clusters of 3-6 at the end of red, glandular, hairy stalks.
**Distribution:** Occasional.
**Habitat:** Sandy flats and lower slopes in the south.

Dec–Jul     Up to 1m

## Hooded-leaf Pelargonium     Wildemalva
*Pelargonium cucullatum*
Geranium family – Geraniaceae

A robust, densely leaved, well-flowered **shrub**.
**Leaves:** Long-stalked, hairy, crumpled-looking, crisp,
round to kidney-shaped, edges toothed and sometimes
reddish, well-defined veins on underside.
**Flower head:** 8–12 large, purple-pink flowers with well-
veined, overlapping petals, in a cluster. Mildly scented
when rubbed.
**Distribution:** Frequently found.
**Habitat:** Widespread. Sandy and granite soils.
**Notes:** A white form may be found occasionally.

Sep–Apr        Up to 2m

## Fleshy Baboon Cabbage
*Othonna digitata*
Daisy family – Asteraceae

A **tuberous, succulent perennial**.
**Leaves:** Green-grey leaves, variable in shape.
**Flower head:** White with purple **anthers**, solitary at tip
of long purple stalks. A **whorl** of green-purple **bracts**
holds up the flower cluster.
**Distribution:** Frequent.
**Habitat:** Sandy places on flats and lower places.

June–Dec        Up to 30cm

## Purple Watsonia     Suurkanol
*Watsonia borbonica*
Iris family – Iridaceae

A beautiful, tall, sturdy **perennial** with a large flower.
**Leaves:** Long, bright green, glossy, sword-shaped, tough.
**Flower head:** Bright purple-pink, mildly scented, funnel-
shaped flowers with wide petals flaring out; alternately
arranged on a green (often purple) stem. Flowers
especially well after fires.
**Distribution:** Frequently found.
**Habitat:** Widespread. Prefers open mountain slopes.

Oct–Nov        Up to 2m

Oct–Jan | Up to 50cm

## Rose-scented Pelargonium     Kusmalva
### *Pelargonium capitatum*
Geranium family – Geraniaceae

A low-growing, sprawling, aromatic **shrublet**.
**Leaves:** Wrinkled, heart-shaped, with rough, irregular edges; pleasant rose-like scent when rubbed.
**Flower head:** Up to 20 pink-purple flowers, with deep red blotches, in a tight cluster at the top of a strong, hairy stalk. Flower heads seem to 'sit up' as though waiting to be noticed.
**Distribution:** Fairly common.
**Habitat:** Mainly lower slopes.
**Notes:** This pelargonium is cultivated for its rose-scented oil.

Sep–Nov | Up to 80cm

## Waxy Satyr Orchid     Rooi-trewwa
### *Satyrium carneum*
Orchid family – Orchidaceae

A beautiful, erect flowering plant on a long, stout, brown stem.
**Leaves:** 2 thick, wide and long, pointed, on the ground; others, smaller, **sheathe** the stem.
**Flower head:** Large elongated head (like an inverted ice-cream cone) covered in dense cluster of pink to rose-coloured flowers.
**Distribution:** Seemingly rare on Table Mountain, although abundant in other places.
**Habitat:** Low sandy slopes, dune-bush vegetation.

Apr–Nov | Up to 50cm

## Persblom
### *Amphithalea ericifolia*
Pea family – Fabaceae

A small, erect **shrublet** with woody branches, hairy when young.
**Leaves:** Stalkless, silky, silvery-grey, hairless or silky hairy above and below, lance-shaped, leaf edges curling down.
**Flower head:** Violet or rose-coloured flowers with a dark violet keel grow in round-headed clusters at the top of flower **spikes**.
**Distribution:** Fairly common.
**Habitat:** Sandy soil among rocks, widespread.
**Notes:** Flowers especially well after fires.

## Slanted Disa

*Disa obliqua*
Orchid family – Orchidaceae

A slender, **tuberous perennial**.
**Leaves:** Clustered at the base of the wiry stem. The growing stem makes a definitive and noticeable kink towards one side, before continuing upward.
**Flower head:** An attractive orchid, pale pink to purple with lance-shaped petals (sepals) about 8–10mm.
**Distribution:** Occasional in Cape Point.
**Habitat:** Well-drained sandstone slopes of the southwestern Cape.

Aug–Sep          Up to 15cm

## Sickleleaf Brightfig

*Lampranthus falciformis*
Ice Plant family – Aizoaceae

A large, diffusely spreading, low-growing **shrub** with reddish stems.
**Leaves:** Small, green or pale green, sickle-shaped, **succulent** leaves with dark tips grow in groups close to the flowering stem.
**Flower head:** Bright magenta-pink flowers with glistening petals and a yellow centre grow, solitary or in 3s, often in big clusters.
**Distribution:** Frequent.
**Habitat:** On ledges or among rocks on mountains.

Nov–Feb          Up to 25cm

## Cape Sweet Pea                    Wilde-ertjie

*Dipogon lignosus*
Pea family – Fabaceae

A small, scrambling **shrub** that grows on bushes and fallen trees.
**Leaves:** Dark green, triangular-shaped, blue-grey underneath.
**Flower head:** Typical pea flower, mainly pink (or purple) with touches of white underneath, growing on a long, slender, twining, woody stem.
**Distribution:** Fairly common.
**Habitat:** Lower slopes in forests, forest margins, undergrowth and scrub.

Jul–Jan          Up to 2m

Oct–Apr      Up to 50cm

## Delightful Heath

*Erica amoena*
Erica family – Ericaceae

An erect **shrublet** with clustered flowers.
**Leaves:** Densely gathered, soft leaves, incurving, pale green with a touch of wool running up the stem, cone-shaped at the top.
**Flower head:** Pink, bell-shaped flowers with a black centre, found at the end of the stem.
**Distribution:** Rare, Silvermine to Cape Point.
**Habitat:** Mountain marshes and streams.

Feb–Apr      Up to 30cm

## Club Heath

*Erica clavisepala*
Erica family – Ericaceae

A compact, bushy, evergreen, much-branched **shrublet**.
**Leaves:** Tiny, dark green, in **whorls** of 4, oblong to egg-shaped, covered in gland-tipped hairs making them slightly sticky.
**Flower head:** Purple to pink, club-shaped clusters of up to 20 flowers at the top of plant stems, usually facing outwards or downwards. Flower is small and urn-shaped with leaf-like **bracts** covered in long, thin, shaggy hairs.
**Distribution:** Rare, only from Smitswinkel Bay southward to Cape Point.
**Habitats:** Sandy, peaty marshes and **seeps** on flats at low altitude.

Feb–Jun      Up to 30cm

## Nude Heath

*Erica nudiflora*
Erica family – Ericaceae

An erect, densely hairy, tightly packed to sprawling **shrublet** with copious flowers in season.
**Leaves:** Relatively long and hairy.
**Flower head:** Small, pink to red, tubular to narrowly egg-shaped flowers with protruding **anthers** grow in profusion at the end of short branchlets.
**Distribution:** Frequent.
**Habitat:** Mountain slopes.
**Notes:** The plant is usually very hairy whereas the flowers are smooth and dry.

## Slant Erica

*Erica obliqua*
Erica family – Ericaceae

**An erect, slender, hairless shrublet, stems simple or sparingly branched.**
**Leaves:** Crowded, erect, scattered, not **whorled**, on thin upright leaf stalks.
**Flower head:** Pink to reddish-purple, sticky, urn-shaped flowers are found in clusters at the top of long flower stalks.
**Distribution:** Occasional.
**Habitat:** On peaty flats, especially in the south.

Nov–May · Up to 50cm

## Red Watsonia · Waspypie, Kannetjie

*Watsonia coccinea*
Iris family – Iridaceae

**A short, rarely branched perennial.**
**Leaves:** Long, slender, lance-shaped **basal** leaves with a prominent mid-vein.
**Flower head:** Pink, purple or scarlet tubular flowers. **Anthers** violet.
**Distribution:** Fairly common.
**Habitat:** Seasonally moist, sandstone mountain plateau areas, marshes and **seeps**.
**Notes:** Flowers more abundantly after fires.

Sep–Nov · Up to 40cm

## Pink Baconfig · Spekvygie

*Aizoon paniculatum*
Ice Plant family – Aizoaceae

**A hairy, trailing or prostrate herb with stems 10–30cm long.**
**Leaves:** Opposite, narrowly spoon-shaped, pale green.
**Flower head:** Reddish-purple flowers, occasionally cream-coloured inside, with flat hairs outside when young; growing at the end of branched **inflorescences**.
**Distribution:** Occasional, more frequently seen in Cape Point.
**Habitat:** Dry, sandy lower slopes.

Jul–Oct · Up to 50cm

Nov–Feb        Up to 80cm

## Sea Rose                                    Teringbos
*Orphium frutescens*
Gentian family – Gentianaceae

**An erect, evergreen perennial with hairy stems.**
**Leaves:** Soft, thick, long and narrow leaves, mostly opposite each other, pointing upwards.
**Flower head:** Large, showy, deep pink (or occasionally white) flowers with bright yellow **anthers** show off their beauty at the tip of the stems.
**Distribution:** Frequent.
**Habitat:** Sandy shores, often near the sea.

Dec–Aug        Up to 60cm

## Beauty Heath
*Erica pulchella*
Erica family – Ericaceae

**A small, bright, attractive shrublet.**
**Leaves:** Green leaves in 3s, erect, relatively short.
**Flower head:** Small, bright, deep pink, bell-like flowers, cluster towards the uppermost ends of slender branches in mass displays.
**Distribution:** Common, especially in Silvermine and southwards.
**Habitat:** Lower mountain slopes. Can grow in large colonies.

Nov–Dec        Up to 40cm

## Yellow-throated Inkflower  Persinkblom
*Harveya purpurea*
Broomrape family – Orobanchaceae

**An erect, slender, silky-hairy parasitic herb.**
**Leaves:** Small, rough, scale-like, pale yellow leaves are scattered along the stem.
**Flower head:** Pinkish-red, with wavy-edged, **lobed** petals and yellow blotches in the throat, grow in clusters of 4–5 blooms on short stalks, at the top of a smooth, rounded stem covered with small, rough, scale-like leaves.
**Distribution:** Fairly common in Silvermine, occasional on Table Mountain.
**Habitat:** Sandstone slopes in sheltered places.
**Notes:** Turns black when pressed or dried.

## Lesser Purple Ragwort      Hongerblom
*Senecio arenarius*
Daisy family – Asteraceae

A small, loosely branched **annual** with a lightly hairy stem.
**Leaves:** Deeply toothed or **lobed**, somewhat floppy.
**Flower head:** Several pink-mauve flowers with yellow
centres, loosely clustered at the tips of branches.
**Distribution:** Fairly common.
**Habitat:** Lower mountain slopes.

| Jul–Oct | Up to 40cm |
|---------|------------|

## Bead Heath
*Erica multumbellifera*
Erica family – Ericaceae

An erect, multi-branched **shrub** in which everything,
apart from the leaves, is reddish.
**Leaves:** Short, thin and narrow leaves, in **whorls** of 4, rise
up the stems.
**Flower head:** Small, spherical, purple-red flowers grow
on a slender stem in bundles, clustered together at the
top of branches.
**Distribution:** Common.
**Habitat:** Silvermine sandy plateau and in rocky areas.
**Notes:** Common in Silvermine, rare on Table Mountain.

| Nov–May | Up to 50cm |
|---------|------------|

## Sandviooltjie
*Lachenalia rubida*
Hyacinth family – Hyacinthaceae

A bulbous **geophyte.**
**Leaves:** 1 or 2 green, lance- or **strap-shaped** leaves, often
with reddish-purple blotches on both sides of the leaves.
The flowers usually appear before the leaves.
**Flower head:** Crimson to red tubular flowers, slightly
banana shaped, with yellowish to purple tips, bunched
together, mostly facing downward at the top of a spotted
**inflorescence** stalk.
**Distribution:** Frequent.
**Habitat:** Sandy areas at low altitude near the sea.

| Mar–Sep | Up to 35cm |
|---------|------------|

Sep–Nov | Up to 40cm

## Sundew Doublom

*Drosera hilaris*
Sundew family – Droseraceae

**An upright to sprawling perennial with an unbranched stem.**
**Leaves:** Many, long, narrowly oblong; covered with sticky, glistening, glandular hairs that, like tentacles, entrap small insects. Leaves turn red in the sunlight.
**Flower head:** Purple-pink (also white) flowers with 5 broad, rounded petals, borne on top of a long, thin, dark red stem.
**Distribution:** Occasional.
**Habitat:** Mostly upper slopes, in damp, sheltered areas.
**Notes:** Flowers open only in sunlight.

Jul–Dec | Up to 2m

## Berry Heath

*Erica baccans*
Erica family – Ericaceae

**A large, robust, sturdy, colourful, bushy shrub.**
**Leaves:** Small, linear-shaped, ascending, almost pressing against the stem.
**Flower head:** Tiny, cup-shaped, rose-pink flowers appear in profusion, on short pink flower stalks, at end of branches. Flowers appear in tightly packed groups of 4.
**Distribution:** Common.
**Habitat:** Upper and lower slopes.

Jan–Dec | Up to 1.5m

## Cape Fellwort Vlieëbos

*Saltera sarcocolla*
Penaea family – Penaeaceae

**A sparsely branched, hairless shrub with slender stems.**
**Leaves:** Grey-green, broad, rounded, leathery, alternately opposite, overlapping, sharp-pointed leaves, often covered with a white waxy bloom.
**Flower head:** Large, bright pink, sticky, glossy-looking tubular flowers with 4 lobes (petals) bending backwards and reddish stamens, borne at the top of a crowded spike. Each head has about 4 blooms.
**Distribution:** Common in Silvermine, rarely seen on Table Mountain.
**Habitat:** On rocky sandstone slopes.
**Notes:** Pollinated by Orange-breasted Sunbirds, a species endemic to fynbos.

## Christmas Berry      Aambeibossie

*Chironia baccifera*
Gentian family – Gentianaceae

A small, richly flowered, multi-branched **shrublet**.
**Leaves:** Small, thin, well-spaced and spreading, growing up the stem in pairs opposite each other.
**Flower head:** Many small, bright pink, 5-petalled flowers scattered around the **shrublet**.
**Distribution:** Common.
**Habitat:** Widespread – likes wind-sheltered and partially shaded areas.
**Notes:** After flowering around Christmas, small red berries appear, hence its name.

Nov–Feb      Up to 60cm

## Narrow-leaved Sorrel      Vingersuring

*Oxalis polyphylla*
Oxalis family – Oxalidaceae

An erect plant with many unbranched stems.
**Leaves:** Has 3–7 thin, parallel-sided leaflets that branch out at the end of leaf stalk, like open fingers.
**Flower head:** Small, single, white to pink, 5-petalled flower with yellow centre, on pink flower stalk. Petals have yellow undersides.
**Distribution:** Common.
**Habitat:** Lower slopes.
**Notes:** Widely found, often regarded as a weed.

Mar–Jun      Up to 20cm

## Purple Inkflower      Jakaranda-inkblom

*Harveya pauciflora*
Broomrape family – Orobanchaceae

An erect **parasitic herb** with a coarse, hairy stem.
**Leaves:** Virtually leafless.
**Flower head:** Pink-purple flowers grow from a stout, erect, hairy stem. Plants turn black when touched, bruised or dried, like ink spots.
**Distribution:** Occasional.
**Habitat:** Northwestern slopes in sheltered, rocky places under **shrubs**.

Sep–Nov      Up to 80cm

65

## King Protea Koningsuikerbos

*Protea cynaroides*
Protea family – Proteaceae

**A large, tall shrub with a magnificent flower head.**
**Leaves:** Large, thick, leathery, somewhat spoon- or paddle-shaped, dark green with reddish edges and long, red leaf stalk.
**Flower head:** Large, bowl-shaped, creamy white centre, surrounded by long, pointed, greenish-yellow or pink to deep crimson spear-shaped 'petals' (**bracts**).
**Distribution:** Fairly common.
**Habitat:** Upper slopes, usually in rocky areas.
**Notes:** South Africa's national flower.

**Jan–Dec**      **Up to 3m**

## Blossom Tree Keurboom

*Virgilia oroboides*
Pea family – Fabaceae

**A tall, profusely flowering large shrub or tree.**
**Leaves:** Many, glossy green above, whitish below; oblong, in pairs opposite each other except for the final leaf.
**Flower head:** Numerous pale pink or pink-white, sweetly scented, pea-type flowers, closely crowded together; in abundance towards ends of branches.
**Distribution:** Fairly common.
**Habitat:** Mainly lower slopes, especially near forest edges and streams.

**Jan–Apr**      **Up to 20m**

## Darktip Heath

*Erica corifolia*
Erica family – Ericaceae

**An erect, hairless shrublet, very variable in terms of its size and floral structure.**
**Leaves:** Green, small, somewhat leathery (*corium* = skin or leather), lie in 3s, close to the stem.
**Flower head:** Urn-shaped flowers, pink below, reddish above, with dark red flower tips, occur on reddish stalks in terminal clusters. The petal tips turn brown soon after the flower opens.
**Distribution:** Common.
**Habitat:** Dry sandstone on middle to upper mountain slopes, fewer at high altitudes.

**Oct–May**      **Up to 40cm**

## March Lily

**Maartlelie**

*Amaryllis belladonna*
Amaryllis family – Amaryllidaceae

An attractive, bulbous **geophyte** with a magnificent flower head on a leafless flower stem.
**Leaves:** Long, **strap-shaped**; appear after flowering occurs.
**Flower head:** Large, fragrant, pink and white funnel-shaped flowers, each with a golden yellow centre; 6 petals flare widely and backwards.
**Distribution:** Rare – found only in a few locations.
**Habitat:** Lower slopes, best after fire.
**Notes:** Good examples can be seen in Kirstenbosch Gardens.

Feb–Apr      Up to 90cm

## Tritoniopsis

*Tritoniopsis dodii*
Iris family – Iridaceae

A **cormous geophyte**, stems unbranched.
**Leaves:** Long and narrow, 1–3 veined, sword-like leaves.
**Flower head:** Dull pink with narrow petals marked with red nectar guides, in a dense **spike**. **Bracts** are short, rounded, rigid when dry. Acridly scented.
**Distribution:** Locally common.
**Habitat:** Sandstone slopes in the south.

Jan–Apr      Up to 50cm

## Grand Duchess Sorrel

**Grootsuring**

*Oxalis purpurea*
Oxalis family – Oxalidaceae

A low-growing **perennial**.
**Leaves:** 3 rounded clover-type leaves, with slightly hairy edges; purplish underneath.
**Flower head:** Small, deep pink (sometimes white), 5-petalled flower with yellow centre.
**Distribution:** Fairly common.
**Habitat:** Lower slopes.
**Notes:** The white variety is found mainly around the Kloof Nek area.

Jun–Oct      Up to 15cm

## Water Heath Waterbos

*Erica curviflora*
Erica family – Ericaceae

A large, woody **shrub** that is often found near water.
**Leaves:** Fine, hairy, small, linear-shaped, in **whorls** of 4.
**Flower head:** Many large, hairy, pinkish-red curved tubular flowers with trumpet-shaped mouths occur, singly or in pairs, at ends of short, leafy side branchlets.
**Distribution:** Fairly common.
**Habitat:** Damp or wet areas: stream banks, **seeps**, marshes or dry watercourses.

Aug–Dec | Up to 2m

## Brown-beard Sugarbush Baardsuikerbos

*Protea speciosa*
Protea family – Proteaceae

A small, erect, multi-stemmed **shrub**.
**Leaves:** Thick, leathery, broadly elliptical, pointed.
**Flower head:** Pale pink and white overlapping 'petals' (**bracts**).
**Distribution:** Occasional.
**Habitat:** Mainly upper slopes.
**Notes:** The only multi-stemmed bearded sugarbush.

Sep–Oct | Up to 1.2m

## Tree Pagoda Maanhaarstompie

*Mimetes fimbriifolius*
Protea family – Proteaceae

A single-stemmed, wide-spreading, green-leaved **shrub** or small tree, with cork-like bark.
**Leaves:** Stalkless, narrowly oblong-shaped with hairy edges; those near flowers are spoon-shaped and dark red.
**Flower head:** Centred among a mass of yellow-pink 'tongues' reaching upwards. Flowers appear white with wispy, yellow, needle-like **styles**.
**Distribution:** Occasional on Table Mountain, but fairly common in Silvermine.
**Habitat:** Mainly the lower plateau, especially misty areas.

Jul–Nov | Up to 4m

## Ninepin Heath Rooiklossieheide

*Erica mammosa*
Erica family – Ericaceae

An erect, colourful **shrub** with many branches.
**Leaves:** Short, needle-like, in **whorls** of 4, pressing
against the stem.
**Flower head:** Dark red to pink (purple, orange-red, green-
cream) flowers in dense clusters at the end of branches;
long flower stalks, flowers hang downwards.
**Distribution:** Occasional.
**Habitat:** Widespread. Rocky and sandy seepage areas.

Dec–Apr          Up to 1.5m

## Wine-rose Heath Wynpienkheide

*Erica abietina* subsp. *atrorosea*
Erica family – Ericaceae

An erect, bushy **shrub** with eye-catching flowers.
**Leaves:** Short and narrow, needle-like, rise up the stem
in **whorls**, curving slightly inwards.
**Flower head:** Reddish-pink, sticky, curved and tubular
in shape with a widened mouth and **anthers** extending
beyond mouth. Grow towards ends of branches:
continuing branch growth occurs above **inflorescence**.
**Distribution:** Occasional to frequent, depending on location.
**Habitat:** Lower mountain slopes, mainly from Constantia
Nek southwards.
**Notes:** Found especially in the southeastern section of
Silvermine in places exposed to cool breezes of False Bay.

Feb–Jun          Up to 90cm

## Buzz Ixia Agretjie

*Ixia scillaris*
Iris family – Iridaceae

A pretty, erect **perennial (geophyte)** with a slender stem.
**Leaves:** Few, long, thin, pointed, with wavy edges,
arranged fanwise around the flower stem.
**Flower head:** Fragrant, 6-petalled, pink flower with
bright yellow **anthers**. Flowers face outwards and are
spirally arranged up a slim, wiry stem.
**Distribution:** Occasional.
**Habitat:** Lower slopes, mainly on the western side, in
sandstone and clay areas. Not found in Silvermine.
**Notes:** Flowers especially well after fires.

Sep–Nov          Up to 50cm

## Sissies

*Brachysiphon fucatus*
Penaea family – Penaeaceae

**A large, brightly coloured, multi-branched, bushy shrub.**
**Leaves:** Dark green, oval-pointed, growing from the stem.
**Flower head:** Small, 4-petalled, deep pink, somewhat rectangular flowers appear in a profuse cluster towards the ends of branches.
**Distribution:** Occasional.
**Habitat:** Upper slopes and summit areas. Likes cooler, sheltered and shadier areas.

| May–Sep | Up to 1m |
|---------|----------|

## Parasol Lily                    Seeroogblom

*Crossyne guttata*
Amaryllis family – Amaryllidaceae

**A strikingly unusual bulbous geophyte with a large, rounded head something like a football.**
**Leaves:** Ground leaves dry and wither at flowering.
**Flower head:** Round, pink flower head, consisting of tiny reddish-brown flowers with 6 small, dark purple, turned-back petals; occurs at end of long pink flower stalks.
**Distribution:** Rare – found only in a few locations.
**Habitat:** Lower slopes.
**Notes:** Flowers only after fires.

| Mar–Apr | Up to 45cm |
|---------|------------|

## Constantiaberg Heath

*Erica abietina* subsp. *constantiana*
Erica family – Ericaceae

**An erect, bushy shrublet with colourful flowers.**
**Leaves:** Green, needle-like, Erica-type leaves (Ericoid).
**Flower head:** Deep pink, occasionally pale pink, cone-shaped flowers occur in dense clusters along the upper branches.
**Distribution:** Frequent, seasonally, in specific locations.
**Habitat:** Mainly found on the slopes of Constantiaberg and Vlakkenberg.
**Notes:** Brilliant mass displays occur on the eastern slopes of Constantiaberg in season.

| May–Oct | Up to 80cm |
|---------|------------|

## Fish Bean

*Tephrosia capensis*
Pea family – Fabaceae

Jan–Dec          Up to 10cm

**A low, ground-creeping, straggling perennial.**
**Leaves:** Small, narrowly oval-pointed, in pairs opposite each other, like oars in a rowing boat.
**Flower head:** Deep pink (purple-red), pea-like flowers that can sometimes be seen at the same time as its numerous opaque, hairy seed pods.
**Distribution:** Fairly common.
**Habitat:** Lower slopes. Not found in Silvermine.

## Lessertia          Harslagbossie

*Lessertia capensis*
Pea family – Fabaceae

Aug–Nov          Up to 10cm

**A small, pretty, ground-hugging shrub.**
**Leaves:** Small, oblong, pointed, occurring in pairs along a trailing stem, with an unpaired leaf at the end.
**Flower head:** Densely crowded, dark red, pea-type flowers, on short, curved stalks appear at end of long flower stem. Uppermost petal is a lighter pink than the lower ones.
**Distribution:** Fairly common, less so in the south.
**Habitat:** Lower rocky slopes, mainly on northeastern to western slopes.

## Climber's Friend          Steekbossie

*Cliffortia ruscifolia*
Rose family – Rosaceae

Jul–Oct          Up to 1.5m

**A robust, densely branched, prickly shrub.**
**Leaves:** Crowded, dark green, overlapping, lance-shaped, sharply tipped, hairy when young.
**Flower head:** Small, nondescript red flower found at tips of branches. Has feathery red stigmas.
**Distribution:** Common.
**Habitat:** Rock faces and ledges, especially in the northern upper areas.
**Notes:** Strong root system, often used by climbers for support when rock scrambling, hence its common name.

Nov–Jan     Up to 30cm

## Blood Bell Heath

*Erica haematocodon*
Erica family – Ericaceae

A dwarf, straggling, hairy **shrublet** with twisted and matted branches.
**Leaves:** Greyish, rough and hairy, glistening, rolled down, in **whorls**. Undersurface white.
**Flower head:** 1–4 small, dark red, hairy cup- to bell-shaped flowers, with a slightly narrow mouth, grow at the end of short branchlets.
**Distribution:** Rare.
**Habitat:** Damp rock faces, usually on south-facing slopes, especially on Constantiaberg and Noordhoek peaks, Silvermine.
**Notes:** Pollinated by insects.

Jan–Dec     Up to 1.2m

## Tassel Heath                    Hangertjie

*Erica coccinea*
Erica family – Ericaceae

An upright, robust and bushy **shrub**, with short side branches.
**Leaves:** Short, needle-like, grouped in little tufts up the stem.
**Flower head:** Bright yellow (or pinkish-red), slightly curved tubular flowers with long brown tips dangle pendulously, in groups of 3, towards ends of branches.
**Distribution:** Frequently found.
**Habitat:** Widespread, on dry slopes in rocky areas.
**Notes:** Yellow form tends to occur in the south.

Mar–Sep     Up to 1.5m

## Coat-hanger Heath               Hangertjie

*Erica plukenetii*
Erica family – Ericaceae

A colourful, tall, erect, bushy **shrub**.
**Leaves:** Needle-like, incurved leaves.
**Flower head:** Large, curved, reddish or white tubular flowers, closely packed together on short **spikes**, emerge towards end of branches and hang downwards. Long brown or yellowish **anthers** protrude beyond end of flower.
**Distribution:** Frequently found.
**Habitat:** Widespread, among rocks on dry slopes.
**Notes:** May flower all year, but mostly March–September.

## Guernsey Lily Berglelie

*Nerine sarniensis*
Amaryllis family – Amaryllidaceae

**An erect, beautiful flower on a long flower stalk.**
**Leaves:** Broad, **strap-shaped**, rounded at tip; appear after flowering.
**Flower head:** Each large flower contains 6 crimson petals with a golden sheen. Petals flare out and curve backwards.
**Distribution:** Rare – found only in a few locations.
**Habitat:** Shady places on rocky slopes.
**Notes:** A Dutch ship carrying Cape bulbs to Holland was wrecked on Guernsey Island in 1659. The flowers grew and were first described there. It is endemic to the Cape.

| Mar–Apr | Up to 45cm |

## Red Crassula Klipblom

*Crassula coccinea*
Crassula family – Crassulaceae

**A colourful, upright succulent with a few side branches.**
**Leaves:** Shiny green, broad, oval-pointed; symmetrically arranged around the stem, in overlapping, alternately opposite pairs.
**Flower head:** Small, bright red-scarlet, fragrant flowers, with 5 curved, pointed petals; occur, densely packed, in a flat-topped **inflorescence**.
**Distribution:** Frequently found.
**Habitat:** Mainly upper slopes. Rocky areas, ledges, crevices.
**Notes:** An albino variation has been recorded in the Kasteelspoort area on Table Mountain.

| Dec–Mar | Up to 50cm |

## Red Disa Rooi Disa

*Disa uniflora*
Orchid family – Orchidaceae

**The largest South African orchid.**
**Leaves:** Long, narrow, bright green, lance-shaped.
**Flower head:** Beautiful and unmistakable, having 2 wing-like, red petals and a raised upper petal (the hood) that has well-defined scarlet veins.
**Distribution:** Rare – found only in a few locations, such as Skeleton Gorge and Myburgh's Waterfall Ravine on Table Mountain.
**Habitat:** Upper slopes. Permanently wet or moist places, such as beside streams, wet cliff faces and seepage lines.
**Notes:** Floral emblem of Western Cape. *Disa rosea* is also found at the Table Mountain aqueduct.

| Jan–Feb | Up to 60cm |

## Summary Snakeflower     Rooibergpypie

### Summer Snakeflower     Rooibergpypie
*Tritoniopsis triticea*
Iris family – Iridaceae

**A brightly coloured Summer flower.**
**Leaves: Basal**, long, narrow and pointed. Usually not present at flowering time.
**Flower head:** Many scarlet, tubular flowers (with 5 curled-back petals) grow alternately at top of unbranched stem.
**Distribution:** Fairly common.
**Habitat:** Upper slopes, plateaux and summits, on dry stony ground.
**Notes:** Pollinated by the Table Mountain Beauty butterfly, *Aeropetes tulbaghia*, which is attracted to red flowers.

Jan–Mar      Up to 90cm

### King's Candelabra     Koningskandelaar
*Brunsvigia orientalis*
Amaryllis family – Amaryllidaceae

**A striking, colourful bulbous perennial bearing a head of irregular flowers; unusual shape.**
**Leaves:** 4–6 dark green, oval to tongue-shaped leaves, leathery with minute hairs above and at the leaf edges, hairless below, spread out along the ground, dry at flowering.
**Flower head:** Bright red flowers, 6cm in length, trumpet-shaped with petals rolled back, in a large, rounded cluster on long flower stalks, towering at the top of the plant to create a candelabra effect.
**Distribution:** Locally common.
**Habitat:** Sandy, mainly coastal areas such as Cape of Good Hope.

Feb–Apr      Up to 50cm

### Fire Lily     Brandlelie
*Cyrtanthus ventricosus*
Amaryllis family – Amaryllidaceae

**An attractive, sturdy, bulbous geophyte with beautiful flowers.**
**Leaves:** Not apparent (dry) at the time of flowering, emerge after the flower has bloomed.
**Flower head:** Bright red to vermilion tubular flowers, widening towards the mouth, are borne on a brownish-maroon **inflorescent** stalk. Some flowers remain erect, others hang pendulously.
**Distribution:** Locally common after fires between December and May.
**Habitat:** South-facing, sandy mountain slopes.

Dec–May      Up to 20cm

## False Heath
**Basterheide**

*Audouinia capitata*
Brunia family – Bruniaceae

A tall, loosely branched, colourful **shrub** with long stems and bottlebrush-shaped flowers.
**Leaves:** Tightly bound leaves press against the stem, giving it a green rope-like appearance.
**Flower head:** Multiple reddish flowers, loosely packed, at the top of stems.
**Distribution:** Rare, seen more in the south.
**Habitat:** Rocky flats and lower slopes, especially in Cape Point.

| May–Dec | Up to 1.5m |

## Cat's Claws
**Katnaels**

*Hyobanche sanguinea*
Broomrape family – Orobanchaceae

A leafless root **parasite** with a tubular stalk.
**Leaves:** None.
**Flower head:** Crimson-red or bright pink flowers that look like a clump of hairy and podgy cylindrical fingers.
**Distribution:** Rare – found only in a few locations.
**Habitat:** Upper and lower slopes, in sheltered areas under bushes.
**Notes:** Feeds on the roots of various **shrubs**, especially daisies.

| Aug–Oct | Up to 15cm |

## Cluster Disa
**Monnikskappie**

*Disa ferruginea*
Orchid family – Orchidaceae

An attractive, **tuberous perennial.**
**Leaves:** Narrow, long, grass-like, **basal** – appear after flowering. Small, **sheathing** leaves up the stem.
**Flower head:** Eye-catching, bright orange-red, open-mouthed flowers crowd in an elongated, loosely formed, often triangular-shaped cluster, on dark red stalk.
**Distribution:** Common.
**Habitat:** Upper slopes, usually among bushes and rocks.
**Notes:** Pollinated by the Table Mountain Beauty butterfly, *Aeropetes tulbaghia*, which is attracted to red flowers.

| Feb–Apr | Up to 45cm |

## Fire Heath

**Rooihaartjie**

*Erica cerinthoides*
Erica family - Ericaceae

An erect and compact **shrub** with a few semi-erect branches.
**Leaves:** Short, needle-like, grouped in 4s (sometimes more), ascending in **whorls** around the stem.
**Flower head:** Long, fat, tubular flowers, bright orange-red with tiny, white hairs; sometimes sticky; occur hanging downwards, at the end of branch tips, in a crowded, rounded cluster.
**Distribution:** Occasional.
**Habitat:** Upper and lower rocky slopes.
**Notes:** Especially noticeable after fires.

| Jul–May | Up to 1m |
|---------|----------|

## Red Afrikaner

**Rooipypie**

*Gladiolus priorii*
Iris family - Iridaceae

A striking, yet delicate, erect **perennial herb (geophyte)**.
**Leaves:** Long, narrow, pointed; the bottom one completely **sheaths** the stem.
**Flower head:** Bright red, with 6 oval-pointed petals and a pale yellow patch at the throat. Up to 5 flowers are borne on the unbranched flower stem.
**Distribution:** Occasional on Table Mountain, but common in Silvermine.
**Habitat:** Lower, mainly southeastern slopes, among bushes.

| Jun–Jul | Up to 70cm |
|---------|------------|

## Lesser Cobra Lily

**Suurkanolpypie**

*Chasmanthe aethiopica*
Iris family - Iridaceae

An erect, **perennial herb** with an unbranched stem.
**Leaves:** Large, sword-shaped, **basal**, **sheathing** the flower stem.
**Flower head:** Single row of large, curved, bright orange-red tubular flowers, curving outwards, each with a long, hooded top petal and smaller lower petals. Flower head bends significantly towards the end of its flowering **spike**.
**Distribution:** Occasional.
**Habitat:** Under trees and damp places on slopes.
**Notes:** *C. floribunda* is similar except it is larger, has a branched stem, and a double row of flowers.

| Jun–Aug | Up to 65cm |
|---------|------------|

## Rock Heath

*Erica nevillei*
Erica family – Ericaceae

A robust, low-growing, semi-sprawling, rock-scrambling, woody **shrublet**.
**Leaves:** Slender spreading leaves, in **whorls** of 5–6.
**Flower head:** Long, sticky, bright red tubular flowers, slightly curved, grow near the end of branches; the **anthers** protrude beyond the mouth.
**Distribution:** Uncommon, confined to a limited area.
**Habitat:** Found on Silvermine's Western Plateau.
**Notes:** Endemic: Constantiaberg and Noordhoek mountains; also found on Kalk Bay Peak on the eastern side of Silvermine.

Jan–May | Up to 40cm

## Table Mountain Watsonia

*Watsonia tabularis*
Iris family – Iridaceae

A tall, erect, multi-branched flower.
**Leaves: Basal**, long, flat, broad, sword-shaped. The leaves **sheathe** the stem closely and catch drops of water.
**Flower head:** Large, tubular, curved, 6-petalled flower, salmon to orange-pink; flowers flare open, funnel-shaped, at the mouth.
**Distribution:** Frequently found.
**Habitat:** Upper and lower slopes. Likes moist or marshy places.
**Notes:** Pollinated by sunbirds. Flowers best after fires.

Nov–Feb | Up to 1.7m

## Common Paintbrush          Veldskoenblaar

*Haemanthus sanguineus*
Amaryllis family – Amaryllidaceae

An erect, fleshy **geophyte** with a stout, unmarked stem.
**Leaves:** 2 flat, rounded, edged with red, appear after flowering. The previous year's dry brown leaves may be seen.
**Flower head:** Large, deep red, circular flower head, crammed with tiny, yellow flowers with bright yellow **anthers**, borne at the top of a thick, cylindrical, red stem.
**Distribution:** Reasonably common.
**Habitat:** Fairly common on the lower slopes in dampish areas.
**Notes:** *H. sanguineus* is also called April Fool.
*H. coccineus* has a stem that is spotted and barred, and longer leaves.

Feb–Apr | Up to 30cm

## April Fool

**Misryblom**

*Haemanthus coccineus*
Amaryllis family – Amaryllidaceae

An erect, fleshy **geophyte** with a stout, pale dull green stem marked with red spots or streaks.
**Leaves:** 2 leathery, smooth, broad, tongue-shaped leaves, spreading or erect, appear after flowering.
**Flower head:** Large red or pink, circular flower head, crammed with tiny yellow flowers with bright yellow **anthers** borne on top of thick, cylindrical stem.
**Distribution:** Fairly common.
**Habitat:** On lower rocky slopes, often in large clumps, especially in Silvermine.
**Notes:** *H. sanguineus* looks similar but has unmarked stem and shorter leaves.

Feb–Apr | Up to 20cm

## Krantz Aloe

**Kransaalwyn**

*Aloe arborescens*
Aloe family – Asphodelaceae

A large, colourful **succulent**, many-branched with flower **spikes** borne in profusion in the Winter months.
**Leaves:** A dense radiating cluster of grey-green, narrow, sharp-edged leaves bend backwards and downwards, showing conspicuous pale white teeth. Leaves form a **rosette**.
**Flower head:** Large striking flowers, mainly scarlet to deep orange; yellow and bicoloured forms (orange-red and yellow) occur rarely. Nectar-producing flowers attract birds (particularly sunbirds) and bees. **Inflorescence** is usually unbranched, with 2 or more arising from a single **rosette**.
**Distribution:** Common.
**Habitat:** Widespread in bush and forest.

May–Jul | Up to 3m

## Rat's Tail

**Rotstert**

*Babiana ringens*
Iris family – Iridaceae

A **geophyte** with a strong, erect, leafless, downy stem, sometimes slightly curved forming a perch for pollinating sunbirds.
**Leaves:** Narrow, very stiff, hairless or minutely haired, pleated, sharp-tipped.
**Flower head:** Bright red with a yellow throat, grow in profusion on a short side branch at ground level.
**Distribution:** Occasional.
**Habitat:** Sandy soils, usually near the coast.
**Notes:** The perch is an elongated sterile flower **spike** that extends 4–5 times the height of flowers, resembling a rat's tail.

Aug–Oct | Up to 40cm

78

## Flames
**Vlamme**

*Gladiolus bonaspei*
Iris family – Iridaceae

A **cormous geophyte**.
**Leaves:** Soft, short, narrowly sword-shaped leaves with a hairy stem.
**Flower head:** 2–7 flowers per **spike**. Orange-red (rarely yellow), trumpet-shaped flowers, often one above the other, pointing in the same direction, at the end of a long, cylindrical tube narrowed in the lower part.
**Distribution:** Uncommon, potentially threatened by alien plant invasion.
**Habitat:** Seasonally damp, peaty sand, both on flats near the coast and at higher elevations in the south.

| Apr–Aug | Up to 50cm |
|---------|------------|

## Marsh Pagoda
**Vleistompie**

*Mimetes hirtus*
Protea family – Proteaceae

A single-stemmed, erect, much-branched **shrub**.
**Leaves:** Numerous large, broad, green, lance-tipped leaves, upwardly overlapping, giving the plant a pagoda look.
**Flower head:** 9–14 tiny white flowers, inconspicuous between green leaves, surrounded by bright yellow, tube-shaped **bracts** with red tips.
**Distribution:** Occasional, locally common near Smitswinkel Bay, also near Olifantsbos (both in Cape Point).
**Habitat:** Lowland marshes and stream banks.

| May–Oct | Up to 2.5m |
|---------|------------|

## Pig's Ear
**Varkoor**

*Cotyledon orbiculata*
Crassula family – Crassulaceae

An erect, evergreen, **succulent**-leaved **shrublet** with a long flower stem.
**Leaves:** Thick, waxy, green-grey, rounded but variably shaped, with thin, red, glossy edges.
**Flower head:** Colourful, bright red-orange, waxy, bell-shaped flowers with 5 curled-back petals hang pendulously in bunches from top of long flower stem.
**Distribution:** Occasional.
**Habitat:** Lower slopes, generally on the drier western side, in bushy places, often sandy and rock-strewn.

| Dec–Jan | Up to 1m |
|---------|----------|

Jan–Dec | Up to 1m

## Red Heath
**Rooiklossieheide**

*Erica abietina* subsp. *abietina*
Erica family – Ericaceae

An erect, brightly coloured, slightly hairy **shrublet**.
**Leaves:** Short, thread-like, splaying out horizontally and curving upwards, rising up the stem.
**Flower head:** Bright red, shiny, fat, somewhat sticky, curved tubular flowers appear in densely crowded, spreading clusters at branch tips.
**Distribution:** Frequently found on Table Mountain only.
**Habitat:** Widespread. All slopes up to the summit. Likes sunny areas.

Oct–Nov | Up to 3m

## Ganna Bush
**Gonnabos**

*Passerina corymbosa*
Daphne family – Thymelaeaceae

A **shrub** or small tree, having slender white stems when young and covered with leaves.
**Leaves:** Long and narrow, opposite, hairy, grooved.
**Flower head:** Yellow and dull red flowers cluster in an oval **spike** at the end of branches.
**Distribution:** Common.
**Habitat:** On sandy, often disturbed slopes, such as roadsides.
**Notes:** Wind-pollinated. Clouds of pollen erupt when the branch is shaken.

May–Oct | Up to 5m

## Common Sugarbush
**Suikerbos**

*Protea repens*
Protea family – Proteaceae

A pretty, robust, erect **shrub** or tree.
**Leaves:** Narrow, long, pointed, somewhat oblong to spatula-shaped.
**Flower head:** Distinctive cream to pink, deep pink or red, bicoloured, shaped like an ice-cream cone.
**Distribution:** Occasional.
**Habitat:** Varied; lower slopes.
**Notes:** This was the national flower of South Africa until 1976.

## Red Hot Poker
**Vuurpyl**

*Kniphofia uvaria*
Aloe family – Asphodelaceae

**A perennial with fleshy roots.**
**Leaves:** Long and narrow, bluish-green, sword-shaped leaves, semi-evergreen.
**Flower head:** The emerging red buds of the flowers, densely clustered on tall **spikes**, gradually change to orange before fading to yellow over time. The red flowers above the drooping, yellow-tipped tubular flowers give a torch-like appearance. Highly attractive to sunbirds.
**Distribution:** Occasional, but prolific after fire.
**Habitat:** Damp slopes and marshy places on sandstone, mainly in the south.

Oct–Apr     Up to 1.2m

## Yellow-eyed Sorrel
**Geeloogsuring**

*Oxalis obtusa*
Oxalis family – Oxalidaceae

**A tiny, bright and attractive flower.**
**Leaves:** Hairy, divided into 3 heart-shaped leaflets, deeply notched at tips.
**Flower head:** Small, orange-pink flower with 5 wedge-shaped petals and yellow centre; often found in clumps. Reddish veining on petals.
**Distribution:** Common.
**Habitat:** Lower slopes on rock, sand, clay or granite.
**Notes:** A yellow form is sometimes found on the eastern slopes of Devil's Peak.

Jun–Oct     Up to 8cm

## Rooisuikerblom

*Tylecodon grandiflorus*
Crassula family – Crassulaceae

**A succulent shrublet with thick, ash-coloured stems, often sprawling.**
**Leaves:** Long and narrow, leaf edges rolled up becoming cylindrical, dry at flowering.
**Flower head:** Large, tube-shaped, with 5 orange petals flaring at the mouth, at the top of an unbranched **inflorescence.**
**Distribution:** Occasional.
**Habitat:** Rocky outcrops, often granite, near the coast.

Jan–Feb     Up to 50cm

81

## Cancer Bush

**Kankerbos**

*Sutherlandia frutescens*
Pea family – Fabaceae

A well-branched, erect or sprawling **shrub**.
**Leaves:** Grey-green, oblong, rounded at tip, slightly hairy, in pairs opposite each other.
**Flower head:** Bright orange-red hanging flowers, open at the mouth; large, smooth, inflated, translucent, bladder-like, pale green and reddish-brown pods.
**Distribution:** Occasional.
**Habitat:** Dry slopes in rocky-sandy areas.
**Notes:** Called Cancer Bush for its supposed cancer-healing properties.

| Aug–Dec | Up to 1m |
|---------|----------|

## Wild Dagga

**Wildedagga**

*Leonotis leonurus*
Mint family – Lamiaceae

A large, tall, erect, unusually shaped, hairy **shrub**.
**Leaves:** Narrow, long, lance-shaped, with leaf edges toothed, saw-like, 'teeth' pointing forwards.
**Flower head:** Orange-coloured flowers, with long, hooded tubes and shorter lower lips, clustered in dense **whorls**, one cluster above the other.
**Distribution:** Occasional.
**Habitat:** Lower bushy slopes, in reasonably damp areas.

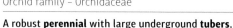

| Nov–Jan | Up to 1.5m |
|---------|------------|

## Ewwa-trewwa

*Satyrium coriifolium*
Orchid family – Orchidaceae

A robust **perennial** with large underground **tubers**.
**Leaves:** Stiff, large, green, leathery, touched with red-purple, **sheathing** the stems at the base. The leaves reduce in size higher up.
**Flower head:** **Inflorescence** is a mass of brightly coloured orange-yellow petals on a tall flower stalk, nodding downwards.
**Distribution:** Uncommon.
**Habitat:** Mostly on moist, sandy flats.

| Aug–Nov | Up to 50cm |
|---------|------------|

## Tree Pincushion

*Leucospermum cordifolium*
Protea family – Proteaceae

An attractive, rounded, bushy **shrub** with beautiful flowers.
**Leaves:** Somewhat egg/heart-shaped, toothed towards the leaf tips.
**Flower head:** Large, orange-red to scarlet, rounded, pincushion-type.
**Distribution:** Only in a few specific locations.
**Habitat:** Does not occur naturally on mountain.
**Notes:** Non-indigenous to the Cape Peninsula.

Sep–Jan | Up to 1.5m

## Cockscomb Gazania
**Botterblom**

*Gazania pectinata*
Daisy family – Asteraceae

A tufted, stemless **annual herb**.
**Leaves:** Narrow**,** often deeply **lobed**, leaf edges rolled down, dark to dull green, rough above and white-felted beneath.
**Flower head:** Yellow or orange flowers with elliptical ray **florets**, solitary at the top of a stout stalk. The flower head may have a dark inner ring with black and white spots and a circle of dark marks at the base. Long and narrow cup-shaped **bracts** occur at the base of the flower head.
**Distribution:** Frequent.
**Habitat:** Coastal flats, low altitudes on sandy or stony slopes.

Aug–Nov | Up to 20cm

## Jackle Inkflower

*Harveya squamosa*
Broomrape family – Orobanchaceae

A fleshy-stemmed **parasitic annual herb**.
**Leaves:** Dusky yellow, densely crowded**.**
**Flower head:** Arranged in a long **spike** of orange flowers with a yellow throat, petals turn black (suggesting the ink in its name) when pressed or dried.
**Distribution:** Rare, mainly in Cape Point.
**Habitat:** Near the coast, from Smitswinkel Bay to the south.

Nov–Dec | Up to 15cm

## Finger-phlox
### Vingertjies
*Manulea tomentosa*
Snapdragon family – Scrophulariaceae

An erect or straggling, grey-hairy **perennial.**
**Leaves:** Small, fleshy, rough-surfaced, shallowly toothed, reddish at the leaf edges.
**Flower head:** Brick-red to orange petals, somewhat finger-like, crowd up an elongated **inflorescence,** with flowers maturing from the bottom upwards. The Afrikaans name ('little fingers') refers to the shape of the petals.
**Distribution:** Frequent.
**Habitat:** Coastal sands, flats and lower **fynbos** slopes in the south.

Jul–Dec          Up to 60cm

## Mountain Dahlia
### Bergdahlia
*Liparia splendens*
Pea family – Fabaceae

A brightly coloured, slender-stemmed, fairly rigid, multi-branched **shrub.**
**Leaves:** Abundant, overlapping, narrowly oval, well-veined, leathery.
**Flower head:** Large, orange-yellow-red flower with numerous long, overlapping, pointed petals that appear to be drooping in crowded cluster at end of flower stem.
**Distribution:** Rare on Table Mountain, but fairly common in Silvermine.
**Habitat:** Grows in the south, on damp mountain slopes.

Oct–Jan          Up to 1m

## Autumn Painted Lady
### Bergpypie
*Gladiolus monticola*
Iris family – Iridaceae

A slender, erect **perennial geophyte.**
**Leaves:** A single **basal** leaf appears after flowering.
**Flower head:** Pink to salmon-apricot flower with 6 pointed petals, the lower 3 having a variable yellow stripe outlined by a pink arrow or W-shaped mark. Several flowers may bloom simultaneously on the flower stalk.
**Distribution:** Common on Table Mountain, but rare in the south.
**Habitat:** Upper slopes, top plateaux and summits.
**Notes:** The only gladiolus endemic to the Cape Peninsula.

Jan–Mar          Up to 70cm

## Common Butterfly Lily          Rooikanol
*Wachendorfia paniculata*
Bloodroot family – Haemodoraceae

An erect, branching **perennial**.
**Leaves:** Basal, long, broad, veined, mainly **strap-like**, with an elongated, pointed tip.
**Flower head:** Multi-branched stem hosts flowers with 6 yellow and brownish petals. Flowers grow and open, alternately, from the bottom of the stem, upwards.
**Distribution:** Fairly common.
**Habitat:** Upper and lower mountain slopes, often in sheltered areas.
**Notes:** Flowers profusely after fires.

| Aug–Nov | Up to 70cm |

## Noughts and Crosses
*Penaea mucronata*
Penaea family – Penaeaceae

An erect, woody, leafy, branching **shrub**.
**Leaves:** Thick, smooth, somewhat triangular, growing directly from the reddish stem, tips outwards; arranged in closely ranked, alternately opposite pairs, giving the plant a square look.
**Flower head:** 4-petalled yellow and red flowers, in a cluster at ends of short **spikes**.
**Distribution:** Frequently found.
**Habitat:** Widespread on rocky sandstone slopes.

| Oct–Mar | Up to 1.3m |

## Dwarf Mirrorface
*Wachendorfia multiflora*
Bloodroot family – Haemodoraceae

An erect **geophyte** with a horizontal, underground stem.
**Leaves:** Long, dark green, broad, lance-shaped leaves, bending backwards and usually higher than the stem.
**Flower head:** 6-petalled, dull yellow to brownish, with green **bracts**, borne on a branching **inflorescence** maturing from the bottom upwards.
**Distribution:** Occasional, flourishes after fire.
**Habitat:** Damp slopes and flats in the south.

| Aug–Sep | Up to 35cm |

## Wandering Jew Wandelende Jood
*Commelina africana*
Commelina family – Commelinaceae

A straggling, **perennial** ground cover.
**Leaves:** Broad, oval-shaped, alternate, strong mid-vein; **sheathe** the flower stem.
**Flower head:** Yellow-orange flowers with 3 petals, 1 being very small.
**Distribution:** Fairly common.
**Habitat:** Among bushes and rocks on lower mountain slopes. Often found near streams.

| Jan–Dec | Up to 50cm |
|---|---|

## Orange Ixia Oranjekalossie
*Ixia dubia*
Iris family – Iridaceae

A small, bright and colourful flower.
**Leaves:** Long, narrow, sword-shaped.
**Flower head:** Bright orange-yellow flower, with 6 oval-pointed petals, sometimes tipped with red, and often with purple or dark brown centre. Petal undersides reddish. Flowers occur at tops of thin, sturdy stems, **sheathed** from the base by long, pointed leaves.
**Distribution:** Fairly common.
**Habitat:** Upper and lower slopes, often bordering footpaths; mainly western side of mountain.

| Oct–Jan | Up to 1m |
|---|---|

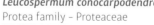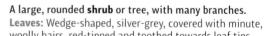

## Grey Tree Pincushion Kreupelhout
*Leucospermum conocarpodendron*
Protea family – Proteaceae

A large, rounded **shrub** or tree, with many branches.
**Leaves:** Wedge-shaped, silver-grey, covered with minute, woolly hairs, red-tipped and toothed towards leaf tips.
**Flower head:** Bright yellow, pincushion-type flower.
**Distribution:** Fairly common.
**Habitat:** Mainly lower slopes, especially in northwest.
**Notes:** Subspecies *viridum* is similar, has dark green, hairless leaves. It occurs from Kirstenbosch southwards.

| Aug–Dec | Up to 5m |
|---|---|

## Thread-leaved Klaas Louw Bush
### Klaaslouwbossie

*Athanasia crithmifolia*
Daisy family – Asteraceae

A large, leafy **shrub** with a firm, upright stem.
**Leaves:** Many, thin, needle-like, somewhat forked or
trident-shaped.
**Flower head:** Mass of tiny, bright yellow, scented
flowers that combine to form a densely packed,
flat-topped cluster.
**Distribution:** Common.
**Habitat:** Upper and lower slopes, often along
drainage lines.
**Notes:** The flowers emit a strong, sickly sweet scent.

| Oct–Feb | Up to 1.5m |

## Foetid Cape Tulip
### Appelkoostulp

*Moraea ochroleuca*
Iris family – Iridaceae

A lovely, erect, robust **perennial**, with a branched stem.
**Leaves:** 1, sometimes 2, narrow, **strap-like**, channelled,
**basal** leaves; bend over and trail on the ground.
**Flower head:** Handsome yet foul-smelling flower with
6 rounded, yellow petals and a deep yellow or red throat.
**Distribution:** Common, especially after fires.
**Habitat:** Lower slopes.

| Aug–Nov | Up to 75cm |

## Common Widow Pea

*Rafnia angulata*
Pea family – Fabaceae

An erect, willowy, multi-stemmed **shrub.**
**Leaves:** Narrow to oval, alternate to opposite on
flowering branches, leathery, blue-green leaves changing
to greyish.
**Flower head:** 1–6 flowers, solitary, bright yellow, fading
to orange and brown, then black on drying.
**Distribution:** Frequent, re-sprouting after fires.
**Habitat:** Stony slopes in the south on coastal lowlands.

| Sep–Nov | Up to 1m |

## Cape Gorse
### *Aspalathus capensis*
Pea family – Fabaceae

An erect, rigid, hairy, thick-branched **shrub**, often in dense clusters, making a mass display.
**Leaves:** Leaves divided into 3 sausage-shaped leaflets.
**Flower head:** Bright yellow flowers, like *A. carnosa*, but with larger petal wing tips. The flowers grow in small clusters, sometimes scattered, flowering at branch tips.
**Distribution:** Frequent on lower slopes.
**Habitat:** Seasonally waterlogged areas in sandstone in the South Peninsula.

Aug–Jan | Up to 3m

## Holly-leaved Wild Thistle
### *Berkheya barbata*
Daisy family – Asteraceae

An erect, rigid, spiny **shrublet** with greyish branches.
**Leaves:** Broad, green, leathery with thorny edges, white-felted underneath; in pairs, alternately opposite each other.
**Flower head:** Solitary, large, yellow daisy flower, with thin, square-tipped petals, occurs at end of branch.
**Distribution:** Occasional.
**Habitat:** Rocky sandstone slopes.

Sep–Dec | Up to 60cm

## Sticky Tar Pea      Teer-ertjie
### *Bolusafra bituminosa*
Pea family – Fabaceae

A twining, scrambling, hairy **shrub**.
**Leaves:** Dark green, broad, rounded, well-veined, tar-scented when rubbed; consist of 3 leaflets.
**Flower head:** Bright yellow, pea-type flowers, with red scratch markings on backs of uppermost petals, grow along elongated flower stalks.
**Distribution:** Fairly common.
**Habitat:** Cooler bushy places on hillsides, often near streams.
**Notes:** Especially noticeable after fires.

Jul–Jan | Up to 1m

## Painted Yellowwort      Naeltjiesblom

*Sebaea exacoides*
Gentian family – Gentianaceae

**A small, brightly coloured flower, often found in small clusters.**
**Leaves:** Small, oval-pointed.
**Flower head:** 5-petalled, flat-headed, bright yellow flower, with 2 short, orange-red parallel lines at base of each petal.
**Distribution:** Frequently found.
**Habitat:** Mainly lower slopes in sandy areas.
**Notes:** The parallel lines are ridged swellings, containing a sweetness that attracts insects.

Jul–Oct      Up to 30cm

## Coulter Bush      Basterkaroo

*Hymenolepis crithmifolia*
Daisy family – Asteraceae

**A soft, evergreen shrub.**
**Leaves:** Large, leathery, grey-green leaves, finely divided into needle-like segments, leaf edges rolled under. The lower parts of the stem and branches are leafless; higher up, leaves arranged alternately on the branches.
**Flower head:** Small, golden-yellow, honey-scented flowers are massed together in flat-topped, dense clusters at the ends of the branches.
**Distribution:** Common.
**Habitat:** Rocky sandstone slopes.

Sep–Dec      Up to 2m

## Heart-leaved Gorse      Steekertjiebos

*Aspalathus cordata*
Pea family – Fabaceae

**An upright, robust, well-branched shrub.**
**Leaves:** Large, prickly pointed, growing out from sides of stem, as though with cupped hands to gather water.
**Flower head:** Bright yellow, pea-like flowers in terminal cluster at end of branches. Flowers go bright orange with age.
**Distribution:** Fairly common.
**Habitat:** Lower stony slopes.
**Notes:** *A. barbata* is similar but has more leaves and smaller flowers.

Sep–Jan      Up to 1m

# Hiker's Horror

*Aspalathus chenopoda*
Pea family – Fabaceae

A large, sturdy, bushy and distinctive **shrub**.
**Leaves:** Hairy, divided into 3 sharply pointed leaflets.
**Flower head:** Bright yellow flowers at ends of branches, in rounded terminal clusters.
**Distribution:** Fairly common.
**Habitat:** Mainly lower mountain slopes.
**Notes:** The flowers are sweet scented, but the shrub has sharp, needle-like leaves, provoking horror in some hikers who touch them.

| Sep–Jan | Up to 2m |
|---|---|

# Common Honeybush     Heuningtee

*Cyclopia genistoides*
Pea family – Fabaceae

An erect, robust, profusely branched **shrub** with tan-brown stem and clusters of bright flowers.
**Leaves:** Dull green leaves, each with 3 narrow (finger-like) leaflets with rolled-under leaf edges.
**Flower head:** The bright yellow, pea-like flowers grow in showy clusters at the tips of branches.
**Distribution:** Frequent.
**Habitat:** Lower slopes in seasonally marshy and damp areas and also sandy areas.

| Jul–Dec | Up to 2m |
|---|---|

# Small-flower Capethistle

*Berkheya rigida*
Daisy family – Asteraceae

An erect **herb**, slightly woody at the base, with creeping underground stems; it can form large colonies.
**Leaves:** Up to 10cm long, blue-grey to green, opposite, white and woolly underneath, deeply **lobed** with spiny tips.
**Flower head:** Small, tubular yellow **florets** in the **inflorescence**, subtended by rows of spiny **bracts**, in small clusters at the top of stems.
**Distribution:** Frequent.
**Habitat:** Clay and granite slopes and disturbed patches.

| Aug–Apr | Up to 1m |
|---|---|

## Coastal Twinleaf — Spekbossie

*Roepera flexuosa*
Twinleaf family – Zygophyllaceae

A broad **shrub** with pale stems and jointed branches.
**Leaves:** Bright green, fleshy, stemless, wedge-shaped leaves, narrowed at the base, opposite.
**Flower head:** Solitary, 5-petalled, star-shaped, golden-yellow flowers with red marking at the centre and protruding **stamens.**
**Distribution:** Occasional.
**Habitat:** Mostly on coastal sands.

Jul–Oct          Up to 70cm

## Fleshy Aspalathus

*Aspalathus carnosa*
Pea family – Fabaceae

A much-branched, erect, **perennial shrublet.**
**Leaves:** Leaflets in 3s; fleshy, cylindrical or tapering, stalkless.
**Flower head:** Bright yellow flowers, growing in clusters, sometimes scattered, flowering at branch tips. The flowers can turn orange with age.
**Distribution:** Common on hillsides and ridges, especially in the south.
**Habitat:** Sandstone soil in the South Peninsula.

Aug–Dec          Up to 2m

## Perdekaroo

*Oedera imbricata*
Daisy family – Asteraceae

A straggling, prickly **shrublet.**
**Leaves:** Leaves dense, spreading, bending backward, oval to lance-shaped, slightly tipped; the leaf edges have small rigid teeth.
**Flower head:** What seems to be a large, solitary, yellow-orange flower is not so. The top of the flower stalk is comprised of many tiny flower heads crowded together, giving the appearance of a single big flower.
**Distribution:** Common.
**Habitat:** Dry mountain slopes.

Aug–Oct          Up to 30cm

## Common Rosinbush      Geelmargriet

*Euryops abrotanifolius*
Daisy family – Asteraceae

An erect, bouquet-shaped **shrub** with few mid-branches and bare stems towards the base.
**Leaves:** Short, ascending leaves, narrow, thread-like, somewhat coral-like in shape.
**Flower head:** Bright yellow, single daisy flower with yellow, spreading petals, at ends of long flower stalks. Large clusters may be seen.
**Distribution:** Frequently found, very common.
**Habitat:** Widespread – particularly on rocks and exposed ledges.

Jan–Dec      Up to 2m

## Golden Head Cape Gorse

*Aspalathus callosa*
Pea family – Fabaceae

An erect, bright green **shrublet** with upward-curving branches.
**Leaves:** Long and narrow leaflets in 3s; hairless, flat, fleshy, needle-like.
**Flower head:** Bright yellow flowers appear in neat, rounded to egg-shaped flower clusters at the end of upright branches.
**Distribution:** Fairly common.
**Habitat:** On sandy lower slopes.

Oct–Dec      Up to 60cm

## Bicoloured Lampranthus      Bont vygie

*Lampranthus bicolor*
Ice Plant family – Aizoaceae

An erect, stiffly branched **shrublet**.
**Leaves:** Cylindrical to 3-sided, rough green leaves with reddish tips.
**Flower head:** 2–3 flowers borne singly or in clusters, bright yellow on the upper surface with scarlet to copper on the underside.
**Distribution:** Uncommon.
**Habitat:** Sandy flats or slopes.

Oct–Jan      Up to 30cm

## Common Sorrel    Geelsuring

*Oxalis pes-caprae*
Oxalis family – Oxalidaceae

A common roadside plant, with many flowers on a long stalk.
**Leaves:** **Basal**, divided into 3 heart-shaped leaflets, hairy underneath, notched at tip.
**Flower head:** 3–20 all-yellow flowers on a single stalk.
**Distribution:** Common.
**Habitat:** Widespread, lower slopes on sandy and clay soils.
**Notes:** Found in grassy places and lawns. Regarded as a weed.

| Jun–Oct | Up to 25cm |

## Yellow Lobelia    Geel lobelia

*Monopsis lutea*
Lobelia family – Lobeliaceae

An erect, straggling **perennial**, much branched, often found in massive clusters sprawling over the ground, rooting wherever the stem nodes contact the soil.
**Leaves:** Stalkless, slender-toothed leaves emerge from red-bronze stems, facing upright, leaf edges flat or partly rolled, mostly unseen, crowded beneath the flowering stems.
**Flower head:** Mainly single or a few bright yellow flowers clustered in **spikes** at branch tops, supported by leaf-like **bracts**; each flower has 5 petals, 3 pointing upwards and 2 pointing forwards.
**Distribution:** Common.
**Habitat:** Damp flats and lower slopes, often along **seeps** and streams in the south.

| Nov–Apr | Up to 50cm |

## Yellow Crassula

*Crassula dichotoma*
Crassula family – Crassulaceae

An erect, single-stemmed **annual**, wiry stems in profusion, branched only at the top.
**Leaves:** Pale green to blue-green, opposite, stalkless, curving inwards.
**Flower head:** 5-petalled flowers in a flat-topped cluster, cup-shaped, yellow to orange or brownish to coppery colour, yellow centres often marked with a red 5-pointed star in the throat.
**Distribution:** Common.
**Habitat:** Sandy and gravelly flats at low altitudes, often in damp places.

| Sep–Nov | Up to 15cm |

Sep–Dec | Up to 1.5m

## Woolly Rosinbush Wolharpuisbos

*Euryops pectinatus*
Daisy family – Asteraceae

An attractive, large, rounded, green-grey **shrub**.
**Leaves:** Greenish-grey, densely woolly; comb-like, toothed like a fern.
**Flower head:** Solitary, daisy-like flowers with bright yellow petals with yellow to orange-yellow centres; borne on long, bare flower stalks. Many flowers may appear on a single bush. Sticky to touch, resinous.
**Distribution:** Fairly common.
**Habitat:** On rocks and exposed ledges.

Aug–Jan | Up to 1m

## Spiny Aspalathus

*Aspalathus barbata*
Pea family – Fabaceae

A robust, leafy **shrub** with an erect stem and wand-like branches.
**Leaves:** Lance-shaped, veined, spiny, bending backwards and outwards.
**Flower head:** Yellow pea-type flowers, turning red with age; nestle in leaves in terminal clusters at top of flower **spike**.
**Distribution:** Occasional.
**Habitat:** Upper slopes, especially after fires.
**Notes:** *A. cordata* is similar but has larger leaves and flowers.

Sep–Dec | Up to 50cm

## Rush-leaved Moraea Geelflappie

*Moraea neglecta*
Iris family – Iridaceae

An erect, unbranched **geophyte**.
**Leaves:** Single leaf, narrow, channelled, cylindrical.
**Flower head:** Fragrant, yellow flower with dark speckled markings.
**Distribution:** Occasional.
**Habitat:** Upper and lower slopes of sand, peat or granite.

## Silver Pea
*Xiphotheca fruticosa*
Pea family – Fabaceae

A beautiful **shrub** with bright yellow flowers, underpinned by silver-grey leaves.
**Leaves:** Silver-grey, hairy, broad, somewhat oval, pointed.
**Flower head:** Bright, beautiful, canary-yellow, pea-like flowers appear above leaves at branch tips in tightly packed, rounded clusters.
**Distribution:** Fairly common.
**Habitat:** Found on dampish soils, often in the mist belt.
**Notes:** Flowers well after fire.

| Apr–Sep | Up to 2m |
|---------|----------|

## Golden Cowcud                    **Beesbos**
*Chrysocoma coma-aurea*
Daisy family – Asteraceae

An easily recognized, erect, leafy **shrublet**.
**Leaves:** Small, thin, bending, near horizontal, growing neatly up the stem. Leaf edges curl slightly downwards.
**Flower head:** Button-like yellow flower, without petals, appears, singly, at tips of slender flower stems. Often found in large clumps.
**Distribution:** Common.
**Habitat:** Upper and lower slopes, sunny areas.

| Sep–Jan | Up to 50cm |
|---------|------------|

## Green Snake-stem Pincushion
### Groenslangbossie
*Leucospermum hypophyllocarpodendron*
Protea family – Proteaceae

A prostrate **shrub** with creeping stems, much branched, reclining on the ground forming a straggling carpet.
**Leaves:** Green, hairless, erect, narrow and upward pointing, much longer than wide, with a finely pointed brown tip.
**Flower head:** Bright yellow, sweet-scented flowers tipped with white hairs, **styles** straight or curving inwards occur in dense flower head, rounded at ground level, sometimes in clusters of up to 4. Multiple overlapping **bracts** shore up the base of the flower head.
**Distribution:** Uncommon.
**Habitat:** Sandy flats and plateaux up to 300m, especially in the south.

| Aug–Dec | Up to 60cm |
|---------|------------|

May–Oct      Up to 50cm

## Fire Daisy
*Capelio tabularis*
Daisy family – Asteraceae

A grey, felted **shrublet** with dense, woolly-white stems.
**Leaves:** Large green leaves on stout stalks, egg-shaped to oval, densely felted beneath, with the leaf edges rolled down, smooth to sparsely toothed.
**Flower head:** Solitary or a few bright yellow flowers on tall stalks in loose clusters. The centre of the flower is tight, while the outer petals of the flowers often arch downwards.
**Distribution:** Frequent, mainly after fire.
**Habitat:** Rocky southern slopes on sandstone.

Oct–Jul      Up to 2m

## Fivetooth Baboon Cabbage
### Bobbejaankool

*Othonna quinquedentata*
Daisy family – Asteraceae

A single-stemmed, erect **shrub** with several slender, branching stems.
**Leaves:** Smooth, hairless, slightly fleshy, wedge-shaped to lance-shaped leaves, often edged or spotted in red and toothed in the upper part, occur on the lower stems.
**Flower head:** Small yellow flowers with neat, rounded petals, set in a small green cup on a short flower stalk, grow on almost leafless branched stems in loosely branched **inflorescences**.
**Distribution:** Common.
**Habitat:** On mountain slopes, often in damp places.

Nov–Feb      Up to 30cm

## Yellow Disa
### Geeldisa
*Disa tenuifolia*
Orchid family – Orchidaceae

A slender, **tuberous perennial.**
**Leaves:** Narrow and tufted at the base with broader, lance-shaped leaves **sheathing** the flowering stem.
**Flower head:** Bright yellow with a slightly hooded upright petal with narrow wing-like petals each side; the middle petal (sepal) looks flat and heart-shaped.
**Distribution:** Occasional.
**Habitat:** Mountain **seeps** and damp, peaty soils.
**Notes:** Occurs especially after fires. Pollinated by carder and leaf-cutting bees.

# Hairystalk Boneseed

*Osteospermum polygaloides*
Daisy family – Asteraceae

An erect, small **shrublet**.
**Leaves:** Blue-green, stalkless, leathery, oblong to oval leaves; tips hooked.
**Flower head:** Single yellow flowers are borne on a long, rough-hairy stalk.
**Distribution:** Frequent.
**Habitat:** At low altitudes, mainly in the south.
**Notes:** Outside of the Cape Peninsula, where plants are generally small, this species grows up to 2m.

Aug–Jan | Up to 50cm

# Sprawling Bush Thistle     Steekhaarbos

*Cullumia setosa*
Daisy family – Asteraceae

A robust, prickly, sprawling, leafy **shrublet**.
**Leaves:** Oval, bending backwards, leaf tips sharply pointed, hook-like.
**Flower head:** Single yellow flower at top of bristly, intertwining branches.
**Distribution:** Common.
**Habitat:** Upper and lower slopes.

Jul–Dec | Up to 60cm

# Rough Ragwort

*Senecio rigidus*
Daisy family – Asteraceae

A tall, sturdy, densely leaved **shrub** with coarse, hairy stems and leaves.
**Leaves:** Heavy, dark green, sandpaper-like, oblong-shaped, toothed; white-grey and woolly underneath, with prominent veins. Edges turn down.
**Flower head:** Numerous small, yellow flowers, orange-centred, massed at the top of the plant, in loose clusters.
**Distribution:** Frequently found.
**Habitat:** Upper and lower slopes.

Nov–Jan | Up to 2m

Jun–Oct | Up to 60cm

## Sea Babooncress
**Bobbejaankool**

*Othonna arborescens*
Daisy family – Asteraceae

An erect, **succulent shrub**.
**Leaves:** Large, thick, fleshy, broadly oval; found clustered around flowering stem, at the base.
**Flower head:** Daisy-like, with 5 widely separated yellow petals and darker yellow centre; flowers borne at top of tall, green flower stem, well above the **basal** leaves.
**Distribution:** Occasional.
**Habitat:** Coastal dunes or among rocks.

Sep–Apr | Up to 1m

## Yellow-tipped Strawflower

*Helichrysum cymosum*
Daisy family – Asteraceae

One of the most commonly found strawflowers – an erect, easily recognized **shrub**.
**Leaves:** Thin, white-felted underneath, leaf edges rolling slightly backwards towards underside.
**Flower head:** Tiny, bright yellow flowers, densely packed in a compact head, appear at ends of tall, grey flower stems.
**Distribution:** Frequently found.
**Habitat:** Widespread, especially on damp slopes.
**Notes:** Perhaps the most commonly found flower on the mountain, in season.

Jul–Apr | Up to 90cm

## Yellow Margriet
**Geelmargriet**

*Ursinia paleacea*
Daisy family – Asteraceae

An erect, branched **shrub**.
**Leaves:** **Basal**, narrow, deeply divided, appearing feathery.
**Flower head:** Yellow centre and yellow petals; pinkish-brown to orange-red underneath, especially at petal tips. Single flower borne at top of long, almost leafless, flower stalk.
**Distribution:** Frequently found.
**Habitat:** Damp rocky slopes.

## Yellow Sorrel           Sandsuring

*Oxalis luteola*
Oxalis family – Oxalidaceae

A bulbous **geophyte**, bulbs large and gummy.
**Leaves:** Small, smooth or hairy, circular divided into 3 wedge-shaped leaflets, often purple beneath.
**Flower head:** Bright yellow flowers with slightly curved petals borne singly on jointed stalks.
**Distribution:** Common.
**Habitat:** Sandy soils on flats and low mountain slopes.

| May–Aug | Up to 8cm |

## Bokmakierie's Tail           Bokmakierie

*Witsenia maura*
Iris family – Iridaceae

A slender, evergreen, woody re-sprouting **shrub**.
**Leaves:** Large, smooth, narrowly sword-shaped, rising upright in 2 vertical rows.
**Flower head:** Several tubular, purple-black and yellow flowers with protruding **style** and **stigma** show themselves in clusters at branch tips.
**Distribution:** Locally common at Cape Point and Silvermine.
**Habitat:** Marshy coastal flats and low mountain slopes.

| Apr–Aug | Up to 2m |

## Painted Peacock           Sterretjie

*Spiloxene capensis*
Stargrass family – Hypoxidaceae

A small, erect, attractive flower with many colour forms.
**Leaves:** Long, thin, pointed, needle-like, **sheathing** the flower stem at the base.
**Flower head:** Single, star-shaped, white or yellow, rarely pink, with 6 tapering petals; centre and petal tips often dark red.
**Distribution:** Common.
**Habitat:** Mainly upper slopes, seasonally wet areas.
**Notes:** The lookalike yellow *Empodium plicatum* flowers in Winter (April–June).

| Aug–Oct | Up to 30cm |

Apr–Oct      Up to 1.5m

## Common Tickberry      Bietou
*Chrysanthemoides monilifera*
Daisy family – Asteraceae

A large, rounded, spreading, semi-**succulent shrub**.
**Leaves:** **Simple**, dark green, leathery, somewhat oval, with toothed edges.
**Flower head:** Bright yellow flowers, with yellow centres and yellow, square-tipped petals; appear in groups of up to 5, towards end of branches.
**Distribution:** Common.
**Habitat:** Mainly lower dry mountain slopes.
**Notes:** Unlike most daisies, bears fruit – purple berries that resemble bloated ticks, hence the common name. *C. monilifera* and *Osteospermum monilifera* refer to the same flower.

Jan–Dec      Up to 1m

## Holly-leaved Kidneyseed
*Nephrotheca ilicifolia*
Daisy family – Asteraceae

A sprawling, compactly leaved, aromatic **shrub**.
**Leaves:** Rough, tough, dry, hairy, broad and pointed, with wavy, toothed edges that roll backwards towards the underside.
**Flower head:** Yellow daisy-like flower with overlapping petals and orange centre emerges, singly, just above uppermost leaves.
**Distribution:** Frequently found.
**Habitat:** Widespread, upper slopes, plateaux and summits, often in dampish areas.
**Notes:** When rubbed, the leaves are aromatic.

Feb–Oct      Up to 50cm

## Common Bulbine      Rooistorm
*Bulbine alooides*
Aloe family – Asphodelaceae

A small **geophyte** with many flowers.
**Leaves:** Long, **basal**, channelled, lance-shaped, often with hairy edges.
**Flower head:** Small, star-like, 6-petalled yellow flowers, each petal having a thin stripe down the centre; **inflorescence** vertically arranged. Flowers bloom and mature from the bottom upwards; each lasts a day.
**Distribution:** Frequently found.
**Habitat:** Widespread, lower slopes, rocky areas.

## Heather-leaved Gorse

*Aspalathus ericifolia*
Pea family – Fabaceae

A tall, erect **shrub** with branches curving upwards, often densely branched. The young branches have a shaggy-hairy or woolly appearance.
**Leaves:** Leaves are divided into 3 segments and are usually hairless or sparsely hairy. The leaf edges can sometimes be densely hairy.
**Flower head:** Single flowers with bright yellow petals emerge on side shoots towards the upper end of branches.
**Distribution:** Fairly common.
**Habitat:** Lower sandy and stony mountain slopes.

Sep–Nov      Up to 60cm

## Lesser Reedpipe     Pepersouskousie

*Tritoniopsis parviflora*
Iris family – Iridaceae

An erect, slender **geophyte**.
**Leaves:** Long, slender, 1–2-veined **basal** leaves, narrow then widening, which emerge before flowering, brown at time of flowering.
**Flower head:** Pepper-scented, small, short-tubular yellow flowers with brown to maroon markings; 2 ear-like petals and 3 smaller wavy **lobes**, spirally arranged in a dense display at the top of a rounded stem.
**Distribution:** Fairly common.
**Habitat:** Rocky sandstone slopes; damp, sandy, marshy places on Silvermine plateau and mountain slopes.

Nov–Feb      Up to 40cm

## Awl Saffron Bush

*Gnidia juniperifolia*
Daphne family – Thymelaeaceae

An attractive, erect, well-branched, spreading **shrublet** with 4-angled stems.
**Leaves:** Narrow, lance-shaped, alternately opposite, hairless leaves are loosely spread up a brown stem.
**Flower head:** 1–4 variably-sized, bright yellow, tubular flowers grow at branch tips.
**Distribution:** Frequent.
**Habitat:** Lower mountain slopes.

Jan–Dec      Up to 50cm

CM

May–Oct · Up to 40cm

## Cape Cowslip · Vierkleurtjie

*Lachenalia aloides*
Hyacinth family – Hyacinthaceae

**An attractive, multicoloured, bulbous perennial.**
**Leaves:** 1–2 green, spreading, lance- to **strap-shaped** leaves with spots on the upper surface.
**Flower head:** Up to 10 cylindrical multicoloured flowers – red and yellow with green tips – hang on long flower stalks.
**Distribution:** Occasional.
**Habitat:** In crevices in the southern granite and sandstone mountain slopes.

CM

Aug–Dec · Up to 60cm

## Sea Cineraria

*Cineraria geifolia*
Daisy family – Asteraceae

**A sprawling ground creeper.**
**Leaves:** Pelargonium-type; broad, deeply indented, with long leaf stalks.
**Flower head:** All yellow, small, flat-topped, daisy-like flowers with 8 petals grow on short stems. Usually found in small clusters.
**Distribution:** Common.
**Habitat:** Bushy and sheltered areas.

BLS

Apr–Nov · Up to 1m

## Mealie Heath · Mielieheide

*Erica patersonii*
Erica family – Ericaceae

**An erect, sparsely branched shrub.**
**Leaves:** Densely clustered, dark green, needle-like leaves, curving inwards, found all the way up the stem.
**Flower head:** Bright golden-yellow tubular flowers, hanging outwards, crowded together on the stalk in the upper section.
**Distribution:** Rare, found in Cape Point.
**Habitat:** Damp or marshy, coastal reed-covered flats.

## Acacia-leaf Conebush

*Leucadendron macowanii*
Protea family – Proteaceae

An erect, single-stemmed **shrub.**
**Leaves:** Narrow, dark green leaves with sharp-pointed tips. Leaves of the female plant usually longer than those of the male plant.
**Flower head:** Male flower heads (pictured here) have bright yellow, tiny flowers in a dense cluster in small cones. Female cones are dark red or reddish-brown, turning yellowish-brown.
**Distribution:** Rare, only one location in Cape Point remains. Replanted in other areas.
**Habitat:** Mainly on damp sand at Smitswinkel Bay.

May–Jun | Up to 2m

## Flats Wingstyle

*Stylapterus fruticulosus*
Penaea family – Penaeaceae

A straggling **shrublet.**
**Leaves:** Leaves opposite each other on long stalks, somewhat egg-shaped.
**Flower head:** Pale yellow flowers with a touch of green, pink tips, surrounded by brown **bracts** crowded at the top of short **spikes.**
**Distribution:** Frequent.
**Habitat:** Sandy flats and hill slopes.

Mar–Sep | Up to 60cm

## Brown-rim Everlasting    Vlaktetee

*Syncarpha gnaphaloides*
Daisy family – Asteraceae

An erect, white-felted **shrublet.**
**Leaves:** Long, narrow, cylindrical, ascending, white-felted leaves with inward-curling edges.
**Flower head:** Fragrant flower heads, yellow to pinkish flowers, cylindrical, disc-shaped, solitary, on long flower stalks underpinned by reddish-brown **bracts** bent sharply backwards, tapering downward. Flowers change colour as they age.
**Distribution:** Frequent.
**Habitat:** Rocky sandstone slopes and flats.

Aug–Dec | Up to 30cm

## Wild Flax
### Wildevlas

*Linum thunbergii*
Flax family – Linaceae

An erect **perennial herb**, unbranched for most of its length, with hairless stems.
**Leaves:** Light green, stalkless, opposite or **whorled** on lower part of stem, becoming alternate towards the **inflorescence**.
**Flower head:** Small, 5 petals, usually bright yellow, but can be pale yellow and rarely white. Solitary or a few at the top of the flower stem. The bud often has a reddish tinge.
**Distribution:** Occasional.
**Habitat:** Lower sandstone slopes.

Oct–Dec     Up to 60cm

## Blister Bush
### Bergseldery

*Notobubon galbanum*
Carrot family – Apiaceae

A large, erect, robust **shrub** with big leaves and a ball-shaped flower head. **Can cause severe blisters.**
**Leaves:** Light green, shiny, stalkless, celery-like with deeply incised edges.
**Flower head:** Small greenish-yellow flowers grow on thin firm stalks; spread out to form a rounded ball.
**Distribution:** Frequently found.
**Habitat:** Widespread, especially in bushy, damp, sheltered areas, such as ravines.
**Notes:** The sap makes skin ultra light-sensitive, so keep affected areas out of the sun.

Sep–Feb     Up to 3m

## Leafless Beardstyle

*Bulbine favosa*
Aloe family – Asphodelaceae

A slender **tuberous geophyte**.
**Leaves:** 2–3 **succulent basal** leaves, dry and thread-like leaves at flowering.
**Flower head:** A few fragrant, yellow flowers with bearded **stamens**, narrow green stripe down the centre of the petal, on a slender stalk.
**Distribution:** Common.
**Habitat:** Sandy and limestone slopes, found more in the south.

Feb–Jul     Up to 50cm

## Greater Rush Iris
**Biesiesriet**

*Bobartia indica*
Iris family – Iridaceae

An evergreen **perennial** with an erect, unbranched flower stem.
**Leaves:** Long, tough, thin, flat, **basal**, longer than the flower stem and trailing.
**Flower head:** Yellow, star-shaped, forming a dense cluster among the spiky leaves, at top of round, robust stems.
**Distribution:** Fairly common.
**Habitat:** Upper and lower slopes, widespread on mountain.
**Notes:** Flowers especially after fires.

| Oct–Mar | Up to 1.3m |

## Sea Coral
**Kinkelbossie**

*Tetragonia fruticosa*
Ice Plant family – Aizoaceae

A colourful, much-branched **perennial**, with dark red stems often straggling through and over other plants.
**Leaves:** Stalkless, oblong, **succulent**, somewhat pea-shaped, leaf edges rolled down.
**Flower head:** Small yellow flowers, grouped at the ends of the branches, supported by **bracts** ranging in colour from red to yellow to green.
**Distribution:** Common.
**Habitat:** Coastal dunes, in sand and between rocks along the coast, and up slopes to 450m.

| Sep–Nov | Up to 1.5m |

## Cape Bogbean

*Villarsia manningiana*
Bogbean family – Menyanthaceae

A compact, brightly coloured flower with unusual petals.
**Leaves:** Large, oval, on long leaf stalks.
**Flower head:** Yellow flower with 5 feathery-edged, fringed petals.
**Distribution:** Occasional, only on Table Mountain.
**Habitat:** Grows in damp areas, often in seepage areas or near streams.
**Notes:** A lookalike species, *V. goldblattiana*, is found in Silvermine.

| Oct–Feb | Up to 20cm |

Apr–Jun | Up to 30cm

## Golden Star                    Ploegtydblommetjie

*Empodium plicatum*
Stargrass family – Hypoxidaceae

A small **geophyte**.
**Leaves:** 3–6 narrow, grass-like pleated leaves appear at ground level, often only beginning to emerge at flowering.
**Flower head:** 6 bright yellow petals radiate from the centre in a star shape, borne singly on a 3-angled stalk. The backs of the petals are green, so that the buds are camouflaged among the surrounding foliage.
**Distribution:** Common.
**Habitat:** Damp flats and lower slopes in open places.

Jun–Aug | Up to 19cm

## Yellow Soldiers

*Lachenalia reflexa*
Hyacinth family – Hyacinthaceae

A short, bulbous **geophyte**.
**Leaves:** 2 green leaves, narrow and lance like, bending backwards, just above the ground.
**Flower head:** Few, erect, bright, urn-shaped, yellow to yellow-green flowers, borne upright on a single stalk.
**Distribution:** Common.
**Habitat:** Damp low-lying places in the south.

Mar–Aug | Up to 15cm

## Cape Fire Arctotis                    Brandblom

*Haplocarpa lanata*
Daisy family – Asteraceae

A large, sun-loving, yellow flower, with crowded leaves at the base of the stem.
**Leaves:** Somewhat rough, oval-shaped, dark green above, grey-white and hairy underneath, well-veined.
**Flower head:** Daisy-type flower with yellow petals and centre; petals are red or purple on reverse. Solitary flowers are borne at the end of long, dark red, bare stems.
**Distribution:** Common.
**Habitat:** Sunny mountain slopes.
**Notes:** Especially noticeable after fires.

## Cape Hibiscus Wildestokroos

*Hibiscus aethiopicus*
Hibiscus family – Malvaceae

A small, pretty, low-growing **shrublet**, with stems lying on ground.
**Leaves:** Thick, oval-oblong, with serrated edges.
**Flower head:** Cream to canary-yellow flower, with 5 broad, overlapping petals and dark yellow centre; borne, singly, on a short stem.
**Distribution:** Fairly common.
**Habitat:** Upper and lower stony sandstone or clay slopes.

Apr–Jan | Up to 30cm

## Golden Spiderhead Gouespinnekopbos

*Serruria villosa*
Protea family – Proteaceae

A **compound, erect shrub.**
**Leaves:** Silky-haired, deeply divided, fork-like green leaves pointing upwards, closing as though to surround and clasp the flower heads.
**Flower head:** A solitary, stalkless, ball-shaped mass of golden yellow floral parts, covered in woolly, white hairs, at the tip of branches. Sweetly scented.
**Distribution:** Rare.
**Habitat:** Mainly mountain flats and slopes at low altitudes in the south.

Aug–Dec | Up to 50cm

## Cape Weed Botterblom

*Arctotheca calendula*
Daisy family – Asteraceae

An attractive, tufted, **perennial shrub** commonly regarded as a weed.
**Leaves:** Basal, in pairs opposite each other, green with white undersides and sharply toothed edges.
**Flower head:** Pale yellow flower with darker yellow inner ring and black centre; single flower occurs on a long, near-leafless stem.
**Distribution:** Fairly common.
**Habitat:** Mainly lower slopes and side of roads or disturbed soil.

Aug–Nov | Up to 20cm

Aug–Sep       Up to 2m

## Sickleleaf Conebush     Blinkblaartolbos
*Leucadendron xanthoconus*
Protea family – Proteaceae

A bright yellow, bushy **shrub**. Separate male and female plants.
**Leaves:** Narrow, flat, sword-like, bending inwards towards tips. Yellow in Spring, red in Summer, silver in Autumn and Winter.
**Flower head:** Cones are yellow or red with a silver sheen; seeds stored until plant is killed by fire.
**Distribution:** Frequently found.
**Habitat:** Upper and lower slopes.
**Notes:** Most abundant protea on the Cape Peninsula.

Jun–Nov       Up to 60cm

## Narrow-leaf Clutia     Bliksembos
*Clutia polygonoides*
Spurge family – Euphorbiaceae

An erect, sparsely branched **shrublet**.
**Leaves:** Lance-like, narrow, leathery, green above and pale below, leaf edges turn down, widely spaced up the stem.
**Flower head:** Pale yellow petals with darker yellow centres; male or female flowers borne on separate plants: males clustered 2–3 together, females solitary. Flowers can vary from yellow to orange.
**Distribution:** Occasional.
**Habitat:** On mountains in sandstone soils.

Aug–Mar       Up to 3m

## Buttonhole Saffronbush     Basbos
*Gnidia oppositifolia*
Daphne family – Thymelaeaceae

A thin, slender, supple **shrub**, found erect or bending over.
**Leaves:** Small, oval, opposite, overlapping, pointed, usually tinged dark red at the tips.
**Flower head:** 4–6 tiny, pale yellow, tubular flowers, each with 4 petals that fold back at the mouth, appear at tips of each branch.
**Distribution:** Occasional.
**Habitat:** Wet places, especially near stream banks.

## Gnidia

*Gnidia squarrosa*
Daphne family – Thymelaeaceae

An attractive, much-branched, willowy **shrub**.
**Leaves:** Small, alternate, narrow, hairless, lance-shaped.
**Flower head:** Creamy yellow flowers tinged with maroon-pink, in clusters at the top of slender branches. Sweetly fragrant at night, unscented during the day.
**Distribution:** Common.
**Habitat:** Limestone or sandy slopes near the coast in the south.

Jun–Oct | Up to 2m

## Tinderleaf                          Tontelblaar

*Hermas villosa*
Carrot family – Apiaceae

A tall, erect, single- or multi-stemmed **shrub**.
**Leaves:** Large, shiny, dark green, **basal**, toothed, with edges curled under, furry grey-white underneath. Carrot-scented.
**Flower head:** Tiny lime-yellow flowers, densely packed in a rounded cluster in a head; forms at the top of a tall, pink, leafless stem, towering above the leaves.
**Distribution:** Fairly common.
**Habitat:** Upper and lower slopes.

Dec–May | Up to 1m

## Wild Currant                        Korentebos

*Searsia tomentosa*
Cashew family – Anacardiaceae

A large **shrub** with pungent-scented, drooping flowers and reddish, hairy-fleshy fruit (the 'currants') on spreading branches.
**Leaves:** On stalks and grouped in threes, egg- or diamond-shaped, sometimes toothed. Dark on upper parts and pale-hairy underneath.
**Flower head:** Cream-coloured, in branched **inflorescences**, with strong smell to attract flies.
**Distribution:** Widespread and common.
**Habitat:** Rocky, bushy areas.

Oct–Dec | Up to 2m

Oct–Jul    Up to 90cm

## Yellow Rice Heath    Geelrysheide
*Erica lutea*
Erica family – Ericaceae

An upright **shrub** with many ascending branches covered with tiny flowers.
**Leaves:** Tiny, linear-shaped, opposite, pressing against branches.
**Flower head:** Mass of small, pale yellow, white or off-white flowers, with 4 turned-back petals; flowers cluster towards the end of branches.
**Distribution:** Frequent.
**Habitat:** Upper mountain slopes, especially sandy areas.
**Notes:** The *E. lutea* in Silvermine are white, except for a few pink-tinged ones on Constantiaberg.

Aug–Nov    Up to 30cm

## Common Bonnet Orchid    Oumakappie
*Pterygodium catholicum*
Orchid family – Orchidaceae

A slender, **tuberous** plant with reddish stems.
**Leaves:** Green oblong, **lobed** with wavy edges and lance-like tips.
**Flower head:** Green-yellow flower, touched with red, cup-shaped, minutely toothed at flower tip, facing down slightly at the top of a loose **spike**. Strongly scented.
**Distribution:** Frequent, especially after fire.
**Habitat:** Damp places at all altitudes.

Jun–Jan    Up to 15cm

## Sour Fig    Perdevy
*Carpobrotus edulis*
Ice Plant family – Aizoaceae

A **succulent perennial** with trailing stems, spreading at ground level.
**Leaves:** Grass green, fleshy, densely packed, triangular in cross section, upward curving.
**Flower head:** Large, single, bright yellow flower with double row of thin petals that fade to pink with age.
**Distribution:** Common.
**Habitat:** Upper and lower slopes in fairly open, sandy, sunny areas.
**Notes:** Often seen on road verges, as a stabilizer.

## Milkball

**Melkbol**

*Euphorbia tuberosa*
Euphorbia family – Euphorbiaceae

A dwarf, stemless, **tuberous**-rooted **perennial**.
**Leaves:** Long, broad, curved leaves, minutely hairy with wavy edges, spread out in all directions at ground level.
**Flower head:** Yellowish-green and disc-shaped, male and female flowers are found occurring on separate plants, above leaf-like cup-shaped **bracts**.
**Distribution:** Common.
**Habitat:** Sandy and stony flats and slopes.

| Apr–Sep | Up to 8cm |

## Green Satyr Orchid

**Soet trewwa**

*Satyrium odorum*
Orchid family – Orchidaceae

A robust, upright plant in dense **spikes**.
**Leaves:** Fleshy, rounded, **basal**, **sheathing** and enclosing stem.
**Flower head:** All-green plant with green-yellow carnation-scented flowers emerging from top of the flower **spike**.
**Distribution:** Common.
**Habitat:** Upper and lower slopes. Found in semi-sheltered, granitic rocky areas.

| Sep–Oct | Up to 55cm |

## Soldier-in-the-box

**Geldbeursie**

*Albuca flaccida*
Hyacinth family – Hyacinthaceae

An attractive plant with drooping, yellow flowers on a slender stem.
**Leaves:** 2 or 3, **basal**, long, broad, light green, deeply grooved or channelled.
**Flower head:** Bell-like, lightly scented flowers with green petals edged in yellow; touch of white on inner petals.
**Distribution:** Frequently found.
**Habitat:** Lower stony and sandy mountain slopes.

| Sep–Jan | Up to 60cm |

## Peninsula Conebush    Rotstolbos
*Leucadendron strobilinum*
Protea family – Proteaceae

A robust **shrub** with a single purple stem.
**Leaves:** Broad, elliptic, dark green, backward-curving at their tips.
**Flower head:** Female: yellowish in green cone; male: smaller, with yellow petals going red towards tip, in smaller, fluffy cone.
**Distribution:** Frequently found.
**Habitat:** Mainly upper, damp, south-facing slopes, among large rocks.
**Notes:** Endemic to Cape Peninsula.

Sep–Oct    Up to 2.6m

## Sticky Green Heath    Groentaaiheide
*Erica urna-viridis*
Erica family – Ericaceae

An erect, sparingly branched, straggly, all-green **shrub** with long bare branches with leafy ends and long, almost leafless flower stalks.
**Leaves:** Ridged, keel-like leaves in **whorls** of 3–4.
**Flower head:** 3–4 large, sticky, pale yellowish-green, egg-shaped flowers, dark green at the tips, grow at the ends of branches.
**Distribution:** Common in localized communities.
**Habitat:** Silvermine, limited to the Muizenberg mountains above Kalk Bay.
**Notes:** Endemic to Silvermine.

Jan–Dec    Up to 1m+

## Hairy-tube Heath
*Erica brachialis*
Erica family – Ericaceae

An erect, robust **shrub**, woody stems branching upwards.
**Leaves:** Ascending spirally, oblong to lance-shaped, densely crowded together, leaf edges rolled under, sometimes hairy.
**Flower head:** Slightly sticky, green, tubular flowers hang down in terminal clusters and gradually turn pale yellow as they mature. The flower tube has 4 shallow **lobes** and is hairy inside and out.
**Distribution:** Rare.
**Habitat:** Granite and sandstone soils on low coastal mountains, some populations at or near sea level.

Jan–Feb    Up to 2m

## Green Violet — Groenviooltjie

*Lachenalia fistulosa*
Hyacinth family – Hyacinthaceae

A bulbous **geophyte**.
**Leaves:** 2 broad, sometimes brown-spotted, like an extended spotted tongue.
**Flower head:** Bell-like, cream, blue, yellow or violet scented flowers, with brown markings.
**Distribution:** Fairly common.
**Habitat:** Mainly lower western slopes in clay soils.

| Sep–Oct | Up to 30cm |
|---------|------------|

## Common Ground Sugarbush

*Protea acaulos*
Protea family – Proteaceae

A small, prostrate **shrub** at ground level that appears to have no stem.
**Leaves:** Erect, variable, large, mostly paddle-shaped, often with a grey-green bloom; the leaf edges and central vein are reddish.
**Flower head:** Large, cup-shaped, yellowish, yeasty-smelling blooms, tips covered in woolly hairs, with the surround pinkish-red at the cup edges. Globe-shaped in bud.
**Distribution:** Fairly common, less so on Table Mountain.
**Habitat:** Lower, dry, stony slopes.
**Notes:** Height refers to leaves above ground, not the flower head.

| Jul–Nov | Up to 20cm |
|---------|------------|

## Green Sugarbush — Groenhofiesuikerbos

*Protea coronata*
Protea family – Proteaceae

An erect **shrub** or small tree with a hairy main stem.
**Leaves:** Upward-curving, spear-shaped, green leaves that become purple-tinged near and around the flower head.
**Flower head:** Large, bright green and white, somewhat hidden by the surrounding leaves. The only bright green Protea with a white bearded tip found on the mountain.
**Distribution:** Occasional.
**Habitat:** High-rainfall areas, lower slopes, eastern areas. Likes clay soils.

| Jun–Oct | Up to 3m |
|---------|----------|

## Green Heath

Groenheide

*Erica sessiliflora*
Erica family – Ericaceae

An erect, woody **shrub**.
**Leaves:** Narrow leaves in **whorls** or scattered.
**Flower head:** Pale yellow-green tubular flowers grow in masses in cylindrical **spikes**. Flower heads retained for many years.
**Distribution:** Occasional.
**Habitat:** Moist flats and **seeps** on lower slopes in the south.

Apr–Sep | Up to 2m

## Bladder Heath

*Erica halicacaba*
Erica family – Ericaceae

A well-branched **shrub** with a thick, gnarled, woody trunk; the brittle branches press against and cling to rocks.
**Leaves:** Finely pointed needle-like leaves borne on densely leafy branches.
**Flower head:** 1–3 large flowers, greenish-yellow turning brown, each about 6mm long, hang down singly from a slender, short stem, somewhat like an inflated bladder.
**Distribution:** Not often seen, but found on Table Mountain and more often in Silvermine.
**Habitat:** Rock crevices and ledges.
**Notes:** Grows even higher than 1m in very old specimens.

Sep–Dec | Up to 1m

## Medusa's Head

Vingerpol

*Euphorbia caput-medusae*
Euphorbia family – Euphorbiaceae

A **succulent**, ground-hugging **shrublet** that resembles a clump of thick, rounded, pointing fingers.
**Leaves:** Has a few deciduous leaves.
**Flower head:** Lumpy cushion-like mass up to a metre wide, with intertwined branches; tiny flowers at end of branches. Has milky latex, considered poisonous.
**Distribution:** Rare – found only in a few locations. A 'special' for anyone visiting Lion's Head.
**Habitat:** Lower slopes. Grows on rocks on the dry northwest slopes.

Apr–Sep | Up to 40cm

## Thistle Sugarbush      Witskollie

*Protea scolymocephala*
Protea family – Proteaceae

A small, erect, well-branched **shrub** from a single stem at the base.
**Leaves:** Long, narrow, hairless, somewhat spoon-shaped, tapering with a pointed tip.
**Flower head:** Reddish-pink to creamy green floral **bracts** cover the young flower heads which open out into a bowl-shaped, pink-tinged, creamy green **inflorescence**.
**Distribution:** Locally common in the south.
**Habitat:** Sandy flats and lower slopes.

Jun–Nov      Up to 1.5m

## Knowltonia      Katjiedrieblaar, Tandpynblare

*Knowltonia vesicatoria*
Ranunculus family – Ranunculaceae

An unusual, nearly all-green flower.
**Leaves:** Dark green, leathery, oval to heart-shaped leaflets with toothed edges, in 3s.
**Flower head:** White to creamy green flowers emerge from a common point on the main stem. Resembles a windmill.
**Distribution:** Fairly common.
**Habitat:** All slopes, in bush-shady areas or woody ravines.
**Notes:** The flowers produce hairless green berries that ripen to black. The Afrikaans name reminds us that early settlers treated toothache with the root of this plant.

Aug–Oct      Up to 90cm

## Green Wood Orchid      Groenmoederkappie

*Bonatea speciosa*
Orchid family – Orchidaceae

A terrestrial orchid with a leafy stem and unusual-looking flowers.
**Leaves:** Soft, dark green, broadly oblong with sharply pointed ends, borne up the stem.
**Flower head:** Few to many greenish-white flowers, drooping and dense spider-like **inflorescence**; the scent attracts hawk moths at night.
**Distribution:** Rare, found in Cape Point (Buffels Bay).
**Habitat:** Sandy soil in coastal scrub.

Jun–Feb      Up to 1m

Feb–May     Up to 1m

## Diamond Eyes

*Staavia dodii*
Brunia family – Bruniaceae

**A densely leafy, willowy shrub, stems shaggy-hairy.**
**Leaves:** Long, narrow, overlapping, closely packed, ascending, with a brown tip.
**Flower head:** Flat-topped, sticky, pink flowers surrounded by a **whorl** of white **bracts** at the top of tall stems.
**Distribution:** Occasional, re-sprouting after fires. Only found in Cape Point.
**Habitat:** Rocky sandstone slopes.

Jul–Nov     Up to 2m

## Teddybear Doll's Rose     Pokkiesblom

*Hermannia hyssopifolia*
Hibiscus family – Malvaceae

**A somewhat twiggy shrub with many long, slender stems.**
**Leaves:** Higher – oval and pointed; lower – larger, more wedge-shaped, toothed, powdery, dry, crumbly and well-veined.
**Flower head:** Many creamy or pale yellow, bell-like flowers that hang from soft, hairy stems; clustered towards tops of branches.
**Distribution:** Fairly common.
**Habitat:** Moist or sheltered areas and south-facing slopes.

May–Sep     Up to 5m

## Wagon Tree     Waboom

*Protea nitida*
Protea family – Proteaceae

**A tall shrub or small, cork-barked tree.**
**Leaves:** Wide, leathery, hairless, bluish grey-green, oblong.
**Flower head:** Creamy coloured, bowl-shaped, resembling a shaving brush.
**Distribution:** Fairly common.
**Habitat:** Lower sandstone slopes.
**Notes:** 'Waboom' is an Afrikaans word for 'wagon tree'. The wood was used for wheel rims and brake blocks for ox wagons.

## Polecat Strawflower     Geelsewejaartjie
*Helichrysum foetidum*
Daisy family – Asteraceae

An erect, robust, unpleasant-smelling **shrub**.
**Leaves:** Oblong, pointed, hairy above; grey-woolly underneath.
**Flower head:** 4–6 large, flat, yellow to cream flowers with creamy white 'petals' (**bracts**), borne in a large, loosely packed, flat-topped cluster.
**Distribution:** Fairly common.
**Habitat:** Damp mountain slopes or marshy areas.

Oct–May      Up to 1m

## Cape Everlasting
*Syncarpha speciosissima*
Daisy family – Asteraceae

An erect, easily seen **shrublet**, with a long, bare stem. **Occurs in clumps.**
**Leaves:** Light grey-green, oblong and hairy, pressed against the stem at the base.
**Flower head:** Single, creamy white, well-petalled, disc-shaped flower, with brown (earlier yellow) centre, on a long stalk. Surrounding 'petals' (**bracts**) are sharply pointed.
**Distribution:** Common.
**Habitat:** Open areas among bushes, on upper slopes.
**Notes:** An everlasting flower when cut.

Jul–Jan      Up to 60cm

## Wit Sewejaartjie
*Helichrysum grandiflorum*
Daisy family – Asteraceae

A grey-white, woolly-tufted **shrub** producing **annual** shoots.
**Leaves:** Crowded at the base of the stem, egg-shaped at the base to lance-shaped at the top, grey-white and woolly.
**Flower head:** Pale yellow to dull creamy white flowers, club-like **inflorescence** at the top of a tall stalk with a **whorl** of white **bracts** surrounding the base.
**Distribution:** Common.
**Habitat:** Cool sandstone slopes.

Dec–Feb      Up to 50cm

**117**

MA

Apr–Dec | Up to 2m

## Black-bearded Sugarbush

**Swartbaardsuikerbos**

*Protea lepidocarpodendron*
Protea family – Proteaceae

An upright, single-stemmed, well-branched **shrub** or small tree.
**Leaves:** Long, narrow, grey-green, upward-pointing, somewhat sword-shaped.
**Flower head:** Handsome bearded protea, purple-black and white head sticking out of leaves at top of sturdy stem.
**Distribution:** Fairly common.
**Habitat:** Upper and lower slopes in **kloofs**, sheltered and moist areas.

HC

Mar–Oct | Up to 1.5m

## Wild Cotton

**Katoenbos**

*Gomphocarpus cancellatus*
Milkweed family – Apocynaceae

A large, erect, leafy, stiff-looking, hairy **shrub**.
**Leaves:** Green-grey, broad, oblong, leathery, well-veined, in pairs opposite, alternately overlapping those below, whitish underside.
**Flower head:** Unusual-looking cream and brown flowers occur in a hanging cluster at top of plant. Flowers have 5 small tubes. Bears purple fruit.
**Distribution:** Occasional.
**Habitat:** Lower rocky slopes.
**Notes:** Has milky sap and thorny, fig-shaped seed pod.

CM

May–Jul | Up to 6cm

## Flat-thorn

**Platdoring**

*Arctopus echinatus*
Daisy family – Asteraceae

A flat-growing, spiny-leaved **perennial** up to 60cm in diameter; a medicinal plant with a long history of use.
**Leaves:** Large, **lobed**, fringed leaves, spreading flat on the ground forming a **rosette** shape; outer leaves on longer stalks than inner.
**Flower head:** Male flowers are cream and borne on short flower stalks; female flowers are greenish and stalkless, enclosed by large spiny **bracts** to form a flower-like head.
**Distribution:** Frequent.
**Habitat:** On sand, granite flats and slopes.

## Rock Phylica — Hardebos
*Phylica dioica*
(Phylica family – Rhamnaceae)

A rigid, much-branched **shrub**, branches buff-hairy.
**Leaves:** Dense, long, fairly large and broad, egg-shaped, rough-hairy above, white-woolly below, leaf edges slightly turned down.
**Flower head:** Many small, white flowers are borne at the end of branches and surrounded by leaves.
**Distribution:** Occasional.
**Habitat:** In rocky places on upper mountain slopes.

Dec–Mar                    Up to 1m

## Rough Chincherinchee — Growwetjienk
*Ornithogalum hispidum*
(Hyacinth family – Hyacinthaceae)

An attractive, sparsely-leaved bulbous **geophyte** with a long stalk.
**Leaves:** 2–4 oval-shaped leaves at the base of the plant **sheathe** each other; those higher up, lance-shaped, wither at the time of flowering.
**Flower head:** White flowers, 6-petalled, with a dull greenish stripe outside that fades to brown. Grow on long flower stalks, collectively forming a loose **inflorescence** of 2–20 flowers at the end of the stalk.
**Distribution:** Common.
**Habitat:** Lower slopes and clay or low rocky outcrops.
**Notes:** Flowers especially after fires.

Nov–Feb                    Up to 45cm

## Flower of an Hour — Terblanzbossie
*Hibiscus trionum*
Hibiscus family – Malvaceae

An attractive **annual** found very low down the mountain.
**Leaves:** Deeply cut, **compound** leaves, in 3 leaflets, varying in size.
**Flower head:** Creamy flower, with 5 veined petals and a dark centre; grows on a firm, hairy stem.
**Distribution:** Rare, on lower slopes.
**Habitat:** Forest margins and damp places.
**Notes:** Not indigenous to the Cape.

Sep–Dec                    Up to 50cm

## Spikeleaf Ragwort

*Senecio triqueter*
Daisy family – Asteraceae

An erect, hairless, sparsely branched **shrublet**.
**Leaves:** Needle-like, sharp-tipped, 8–15mm long.
**Flower head:** Solitary **inflorescence** at the top of slender stalk, cream to yellow with protruding **stamens**, surrounded below by a circle of greening **bracts**.
**Distribution:** Occasional.
**Habitat:** On rocky slopes in the south.

Jan–May          Up to 30cm

## Hooks Buchu

*Agathosma hookeri*
Citrus family – Rutaceae

A low-spreading **shrublet**.
**Leaves:** Narrow, rounded, hairy green leaves rising in whorls.
**Flower head:** Yellowish-cream flowers in a cluster at the tip of the stem. Flower has a faint buchu smell.
**Distribution:** Rare, found in Cape Point.
**Habitat:** Sandy flats at foot of mountains.

Aug–Nov          Up to 30cm

## Fragrant Crassula          Klipblom

*Crassula fascicularis*
Crassula family – Crassulaceae

A small, erect, **perennial succulent**.
**Leaves:** Small, lance-shaped, semi-**succulent**, hairy-edged, ascending the red stem.
**Flower head:** Jasmine-like flowers, white, cream, or pinkish, loosely clustered together in a rounded to flat-topped, multi-flowered **inflorescence**, like a bouquet, at end of flower stem. Scented in evening.
**Distribution:** Fairly common.
**Habitat:** Mainly lower slopes, especially sandstone.
**Notes:** Buds appear dull red.

Sep–Dec          Up to 40cm

## Golden Disa

*Disa cornuta*
Orchid family – Orchidaceae

Oct–Feb          Up to 50cm

A sturdy, upright or semi-erect **tuberous perennial**.
**Leaves:** Large, broad, overlapping, pointed, tapering in size from the bottom up; streaked with red blotches, they **sheathe** the stem.
**Flower head:** Unusually attractive, multi-flowered **spike** with distinctive colouring: each flower has a purple-mauve hood, white inside with a purple-black centre spot.
**Distribution:** Rare – found only in a few locations.
**Habitat:** Upper slopes, among **shrubs**, in sandy areas, usually in high-rainfall areas.
**Notes:** Faintly spice-scented. Also nicknamed the 'Inkspot Disa'.

## Featherhead                    Veerkoppie

*Phylica pubescens*
Phylica family – Rhamnaceae

Apr–Dec          Up to 2m

An attractive **shrub**, densely covered with soft, feathery, unmatted hairs.
**Leaves:** Grey-green, narrow, hairy, pointed; edges turn downwards.
**Flower head:** Pale to creamy yellow, fluffy flowers in a solitary flower head; resembles a small feather duster.
**Distribution:** Occasional.
**Habitat:** Mainly lower eastern slopes.

## Curly-leaved Strawflower

*Helichrysum patulum*
Daisy family – Asteraceae

Sep–Feb          Up to 70cm

A straggling, much-branched, woolly **shrub** or **shrublet**.
**Leaves:** Stalkless, white-woolly, paddle-shaped; spaced out up a stout flower stem.
**Flower head:** Bell-shaped, pale yellow flowers, ringed by white round-tipped **bracts**, cluster in a mass display at the top of the flower stalk.
**Distribution:** Common.
**Habitat:** In localized patches on open parts of the mountain and vlei edges.

## Helichrysum
### *Helichrysum fruticans*
Daisy family – Asteraceae

**An erect, woolly shrub with multiple flower heads.**
**Leaves:** Broad, oval, grey-green, woolly.
**Flower head:** White flowers with yellow centres, crowded together in a large, tightly bunched head, at end of an almost naked flower stem.
**Distribution:** Frequently found.
**Habitat:** Upper and lower slopes.

Sep–Feb                    Up to 50cm

## Common Button Daisy                    Ganskos
### *Cotula turbinata*
Daisy family – Asteraceae

**An unmistakable, softly hairy annual that flowers early.**
**Leaves:** Small, low growing, feathery grey-green, on alternate sides of stem; finely twice- or thrice-divided.
**Flower head:** Single, yellow-centred flower with tiny white or yellow petals, on slender flower stalk. Often found in clumps.
**Distribution:** Common.
**Habitat:** Widespread, mainly lower slopes, sunny areas.
**Notes:** Often regarded as a weed.

Jul–Nov                    Up to 30cm

## Arctotis                    Taaigousblom
### *Arctotis aspera*
Daisy family – Asteraceae

**A sprawling shrub with a leafy stem.**
**Leaves:** Irregularly shaped, deeply lobed, hairy, covered with bristles.
**Flower head:** Single daisy flower with white petals (red to purple underside) and yellow centre, on a green flower stalk.
**Distribution:** Fairly common.
**Habitat:** Mountain slopes; widespread, especially in the drier northern areas.

Aug–Oct                    Up to 1m

## Silver Arctotis

**Duine Gousblom**

*Arctotis stoechadifolia*
Daisy family – Asteraceae

A tough, sprawling, fast-growing ground cover, often seen in gardens around the world.
**Leaves:** Soft, silvery, felted leaves; **lobed**, long and narrow, with the edges slightly toothed. Leaves are sticky when touched and emit a strong, bittersweet smell.
**Flower head:** Creamy white to light yellow petals and a dark disc centre; undersides of the petals are reddish-maroon. The **bracts** are thin and woolly with papery edges.
**Distribution:** Rare.
**Habitat:** Occurs naturally along a small strip from Table Bay to Cape Point.

| Sep–Dec | Up to 35cm |
|---|---|

## Chincherinchee

**Tjienk**

*Ornithogalum thyrsoides*
Hyacinth family – Hyacinthaceae

A popular, commercially sold, bulbous **perennial**.
**Leaves:** **Basal**, broad, lance-shaped and often leaning outwards; have slightly hairy edges. Sometimes dry at time of flowering.
**Flower head:** Large, creamy white, bowl-shaped flowers with 6 oval-pointed petals, often with green-brown centres that fade with age; grow together in tightly bunched clusters, at the top of flower stems.
**Distribution:** Fairly common.
**Habitat:** Damp, partly shady, sandy places on lower slopes.

| Oct–Dec | Up to 80cm |
|---|---|

## Sea Strawflower

*Helichrysum retortum*
Daisy family – Asteraceae

A straggling, closely leafy, silvery **shrublet**.
**Leaves:** Small, overlapping, oblong, channelled, covered with tissue paper-like hairs, upper leaves curled back, hooked at the tips.
**Flower head:** White everlasting (papery) flowers with yellow centres, solitary at the stem tips, surrounded by hairless, white glossy **bracts**, pink to brown on the outer surface.
**Distribution:** Common.
**Habitat:** Cliffs above the seashore, coastal dunes or sandy flats and slopes close to the sea.

| Aug–Dec | Up to 50cm |
|---|---|

## Common Paperflower · Sewejaartjie
*Edmondia sesamoides*
Daisy family – Asteraceae

An erect, lightly branched **shrublet** with a grey-white stem.
**Leaves: Basal**, narrow, lying open, leaf edges curling up; higher: small, overlapping, pressing against flower stem.
**Flower head:** Central part white (or yellow), surrounded by layers of silky white (or pink), reflective, papery petals. Pink in bud.
**Distribution:** Common.
**Habitat:** Open sunny areas.

Aug–Jan          Up to 40cm

## Cape Geranium · Vrouebossie
*Geranium incanum*
Geranium family – Geraniaceae

A widely spreading ground cover; an evergreen **perennial** with multi-branched stems.
**Leaves:** Thin, much divided, green above, grey below, on long leaf stalks.
**Flower head:** White, 5 broad petals with marked veins; usually solitary, appear on thin stalks above leaves. Petals have a notch, or dent, at their tips.
**Distribution:** Rare – found only in a few locations.
**Habitat:** Sandy and stony soils.
**Notes:** Flowers can be purple or pink, variable in size.

Aug–Nov          Up to 30cm

## Arum Lily · Varkblom
*Zantedeschia aethiopica*
Arum family – Araceae

A handsome, well-known white flower.
**Leaves:** Dark green, broadly arrowhead-shaped, on long, spongy leaf stalks.
**Flower head:** Single, large, white petal surrounds a small central yellow column. Often found in clumps.
**Distribution:** Fairly common.
**Habitat:** Seasonally damp, shady, sheltered areas, among rocks and bushes.
**Notes:** Wild porcupines eat the bulb.

Jun–Dec          Up to 1.2m

## Common Sunshine Conebush    Geelbos
*Leucadendron salignum*
Protea family – Proteaceae

**A small, variable, multi-stemmed plant.**
**Leaves:** Long, smooth, narrow, pointed, alternate, twisting. During flowering, upper leaves turn ivory, yellow or red.
**Flower head:** Distinguished from other multi-stemmed Sunshine Conebushes by its silver-grey cones, and the conspicuous cup around the cones.
**Distribution:** Fairly common.
**Habitat:** Upper and lower slopes, in open sunny areas.
**Notes:** The most widespread *Leucadendron* in South Africa.

Apr–Nov                    Up to 50cm

## Cape Heath
*Erica capensis*
Erica family – Ericaceae

**An erect, branching species of Erica.**
**Leaves:** Light green, thin leaves in **whorls**, upright to splayed, occur on firm, branching stems.
**Flower head:** Small, cup-shaped, white or pink flowers are found in profusion in tight clusters.
**Distribution:** Rare.
**Habitat:** Endemic to low, marshy areas of Cape Point.

Dec–Apr                    Up to 50cm

## Marsh Bulbinella    Katstert
*Bulbinella nutans*
Aloe family – Asphodelaceae

**A tall, perennial herb.**
**Leaves:** Bright green, long, **strap-like**, channelled.
**Flower head:** Mass of white and yellow (rarely orange), unscented flowers, in an elongated head, at end of long, green, leafless flower stem. Often found in clumps. Flowers are short lived.
**Distribution:** Fairly common on Table Mountain.
**Habitat:** Occurs in moist areas such as stream banks, **seeps** and soggy soils.

Sep–Oct                    Up to 1m

125

## Silver Tree             Witteboom

*Leucadendron argenteum*
Protea family – Proteaceae

A handsome tree with a stout trunk, thick, grey-coloured bark and silvery-looking leaves. Separate male and female plants.
**Leaves:** Soft, shiny, green-grey, long, tapering, covered with fine silvery hairs.
**Flower head:** Female identified by a large, silver, egg-shaped cone surrounded by long leaves; male (shown here) is considerably smaller and less obvious.
**Distribution:** Occasional.
**Habitat:** Lower sunny slopes, mainly forest margins; damp, granite and clay soils.
**Notes:** Endangered. Endemic to the Peninsula.

Sep–Oct             Up to 10m

## Common Starheath        Altydbos

*Staavia radiata*
Brunia family – Bruniaceae

An erect **shrublet** with a leafy stem and short, thin branchlets.
**Leaves:** Small, narrow, lance-shaped, brown-tipped, pointing upwards.
**Flower head:** Tiny, white, daisy-like flower with dark red-purple centre. Often found in clumps.
**Distribution:** Occasional.
**Habitat:** Widespread, often found on sandy soils and dampish areas.

Sep–Dec             Up to 60cm

## African Stachys           Katbossie

*Stachys aethiopica*
Mint family – Lamiaceae

A sprawling **perennial** with bristly 4-sided stems.
**Leaves:** Egg-shaped to triangular, toothed.
**Flower head:** **Whorls** of 2–6 white or pink to mauve flowers with darker spots.
**Distribution:** Frequent.
**Habitat:** Often in shade in **fynbos** and forest edges.
**Notes:** Also commonly called teebos and woundwort.

Aug–May             Up to 50cm

## Anaxeton

*Anaxeton laeve*
Daisy family – Asteraceae

A small, woolly **shrublet** with a long flower stalk.
**Leaves:** Thin, stalkless, upward curving, grey-green, with shiny upper surfaces and woolly underneath.
**Flower head:** Small, red-backed flowers in bud, densely packed in a tight, round-headed cluster, turning white when open.
**Distribution:** Frequently found.
**Habitat:** Widespread, mainly upper slopes, but also plateaux and summits.

Apr–Oct                    Up to 45m

## Ash Flower                    Wilde Sewejaartjie

*Petalacte coronata*
Daisy family – Asteraceae

An attractive, small, low-growing, greyish-white, sparsely branched, intensely woolly plant with white flowers.
**Leaves:** Semi-erect, inversely lance-shaped.
**Flower head:** Looks like ultra-miniature white roses; the grey-white flowers are borne in a round flower cluster.
**Distribution:** Frequent in Silvermine; occasional on Table Mountain.
**Habitat:** On dry sandstone slopes.

Jun–Oct                    Up to 50cm

## Dune Celery                    Duineseldery

*Dasispermum suffruticosum*
Carrot family – Apiaceae

A short-lived, prostrate **perennial** with a woody base that sprawls across sand dunes.
**Leaves:** Leathery and fleshy, up to 8cm long, narrow, toothed, twice-divided leaflets, curled inward. The leaves resemble parsley.
**Flower head:** Small white to cream-coloured flowers with yellow centres appear at the top of a thick stalk in wide, spreading, flat-topped to curving clusters up to 30mm across, double that when fruiting.
**Distribution:** Locally common in Cape Point.
**Habitat:** Dunes and sandy slopes.

Jan–Dec                    Up to 50cm

Oct–Dec          Up to 30m

## Bladder Cell Stonecrop

*Crassula pruinosa*
Crassula family – Crassulaceae

A slightly woody **perennial** with hairy backward-bending branches when young; wiry stems and attractive flowers.
**Leaves:** Dull green, stalkless, widely spaced, alternately opposite, somewhat lance-shaped leaves grow up a brown stem.
**Flower head:** Many white tubular flowers in a flat-topped cluster with prominent red **stamens**; yellow when still opening.
**Distribution:** Occasional.
**Habitat:** Rocky areas on the lower slopes.

Aug–Jan          Up to 70cm

## Blombos

*Metalasia divergens*
Daisy family – Asteraceae

A sprawling, white-woolly, densely leaved **shrublet**.
**Leaves:** Long, slightly twisted and bending backwards.
**Flower head:** Small white or pink flowers combine in dense terminal clusters to form a disc-shaped 'head'. The outer **bracts** are brown to reddish.
**Distribution:** Common.
**Habitat:** Southern sandstone slopes.

May–Dec          Up to 60cm

## Box Heath

*Erica pyxidiflora*
Erica family – Ericaceae

An erect **shrublet** with a cylindrical head; upright, hairless branches and copious leaves.
**Leaves:** Short, thick, hairy, inward curving; ascending in 6s that densely crowd the topmost branches from which flowers emerge.
**Flower head:** Stalkless, pale pink to white urn-shaped flowers with a wide, rounded mouth showing dark **anthers**, emerge through the leaves of long, erect branches.
**Distribution:** Occasional
**Habitat:** Found in damp, soggy or marshy conditions and near streams on Table Mountain and in Silvermine, such as on the Steenberg Plateau.

## Calycina
*Erica calycina*
Erica family – Ericaceae

An erect **shrublet** with many semi-erect, rigid branches.
**Leaves:** Small, linear-shaped, ascending, tightly packed, in groups of 3.
**Flower head:** Showy, plentiful, white, bell-shaped flowers with dusky 'mouths' (caused by dark **anthers**), in groups of 3, at end of small branches.
**Distribution:** Frequently found.
**Habitat:** Upper slopes and summits, rocky areas.

Jul–Dec                    Up to 2m

## Cape Snow                    Witsewejaartjie
*Syncarpha vestita*
Daisy family – Asteraceae

A compact, multi-branched, densely leaved **shrub**.
**Leaves:** Ascending, woolly grey-green, long, **strap-like**, overlapping, dark-tipped.
**Flower head:** Large, rounded, 'everlasting' flower with papery, white, pointed 'petals' (**bracts**) and purple-red centre that goes brown with age. Flower is borne on a sturdy, grey, woolly stem.
**Distribution:** Fairly common.
**Habitat:** Upper slopes.
**Notes:** The flowers, when cut, last more or less for ever.

Oct–Jan                    Up to 1m

## Cape Snowdrop                    Skaamblommetjie
*Crassula capensis*
Crassula family – Crassulaceae

A small, delicate, erect, **tuberous perennial**.
**Leaves:** Relatively large, green with purple underneath, rounded, ground-hugging, with a scalloped edge.
**Flower head:** Small, snowy white, cup-shaped, 6-petalled flowers on red flower stalks; form in a loose cluster at the top of a **spike**. Some flowers bend over and droop.
**Distribution:** Occasional.
**Habitat:** Occurs in sheltered damp areas.

Jun–Aug                    Up to 15cm

**129**

CM

Aug–Oct     Up to 50cm

## China Flower     Bergskaapboegoe
*Adenandra uniflora*
Citrus family – Rutaceae

An evergreen, sparsely branched, aromatic **shrublet**.
**Leaves:** Small, soft, oval, with rolled-down edges. Spot markings on leaves.
**Flower head:** Single flower, glistening white, 5 rounded petals with red centre and veins. Undersides pink. Red buds.
**Distribution:** Frequently found.
**Habitat:** Mainly lower slopes, in northwestern drier areas.
**Notes:** Lookalike *A. villosa* is taller, bears clusters of flowers; flat leaves, often hairy on underside.

HC

Jun–Dec     Up to 2m

## Common Buttonbush     Vleiknoppiesbos
*Berzelia lanuginosa*
Brunia family – Bruniaceae

A large, evergreen, densely leaved, multi-branched **shrub**.
**Leaves:** Tiny, thin, black-tipped, upward curving; press against soft flexible branches.
**Flower head:** Tiny, creamy white, fluffy, ball-shaped flowers grow profusely in tight clusters at branch tips and go brown with age.
**Distribution:** Frequently found.
**Habitat:** Damp slopes, stream banks, and near water.
**Notes:** Similar to *Brunia noduliflora* but flower heads smaller, leaves softer when brushed.

GN

Jun–Dec     Up to 1.8m

## Confetti Bush     Klipboegoe
*Coleonema album*
Citrus family – Rutaceae

A large, erect, multi-branched, rounded, bushy **shrub**.
**Leaves:** Small, alternate, narrow and copious. The gland-dotted leaves rise up the reddish branch stems.
**Flower head:** Mass of small, white, sweet-scented flowers with dark green centres, spread – like thrown confetti – over the bush at branch tips. Petals veined with pink; buds pinkish.
**Distribution:** Common.
**Habitat:** Found especially among granite outcrops and rocky ledges.

## Klipblom

*Crassula obtusa*
Crassula family - Crassulaceae

A sprawling **perennial shrublet**, branches short, reclining on the ground, often rooting where touching ground.
**Leaves:** Oblong to paddle-shaped with hairy edges, varying in colour from green to brown or red.
**Flower head:** 1–5 white, 5-petalled flowers with black **anthers**, often tinged pink or red, darkening with age.
**Distribution:** Common, widespread.
**Habitat:** Moist sandstone, mainly in the south.

Nov–Feb          Up to 15cm

## Dark-eyed Ixia

*Ixia polystachya*
Iris family - Iridaceae

A tall, slender **geophyte** with 1–4 branched stems carrying a **spike** of flowers of variable coloration.
**Leaves:** Variable in size and shape, often long and narrow, lance- to sword-shaped.
**Flower head:** 1 to many, faintly scented, 6-petalled flowers, usually white, but also in shades of pink, mauve, or purple, are borne at the top of a lax **spike**. The flower centres can be green, blue, purple, pink, yellow or white.
**Distribution:** Frequent on Table Mountain, less common in the south; favours eastern slopes.
**Habitat:** Damp or shady areas on sandstone or granite soils on the mountain and flats.

Oct–Dec          Up to 80cm

## Disa

*Disa bivalvata*
Orchid family - Orchidaceae

A slight, robust **perennial**.
**Leaves:** Small, narrow to lance-like, arising from the stem, tuft-like.
**Flower head:** The **inflorescence** is a tight, flat-topped cluster of up to 30 bicoloured flowers, the sepals white, and the petals and lip pale to dark maroon. The flowers are arranged in a horizontal circle to mimic female wasps. The scent mimics that of female wasps, attracting male wasps who pollinate the flowers.
**Distribution:** Locally abundant, usually after fire.
**Habitat:** Marshes, damp mountain slopes and **seeps**.

Sep–Jan          Up to 45cm

131

Mar–Jun    Up to 50cm

## Dogface    Hondegesig

*Trichocephalus stipularis*
Phylica family – Rhamnaceae

A stout, much-branched **shrublet** with a dark-coloured stem.
**Leaves:** Long, narrow, alternate, ascending, lance-shaped; leaf edges rolled down.
**Flower head:** Solitary, small, honey-scented pink flowers, densely woolly-white on the outside, are borne at the top of thick, branched stems. Flowers are tightly clustered together.
**Distribution:** Common.
**Habitat:** Sandy lower slopes.

Sep–Oct    Up to 30cm

## Gifbol

*Drimia filifolia*
Hyacinth family – Hyacinthaceae

A bulbous **geophyte.**
**Leaves:** Few leaves approximately 1mm in diameter, present at flowering, drying out during the summer months.
**Flower head:** Star-shaped, white flowers with green stripes often flushed purple, sweetly fragrant, appearing in a small cluster at the top of a long, banded sheath.
**Distribution:** Occasional, but frequent after fire.
**Habitat:** Sandy slopes and flats, clay soils.

Jun–Nov    Up to 40cm

## Drumsticks    Verfblommetjie

*Zaluzianskya capensis*
Sutera family – Scrophulariaceae

A short-lived **annual** whose flowers, resembling kettledrum sticks, remain closed during the day and open at night.
**Leaves:** Tiny, narrow, irregularly edged, stalkless.
**Flower head:** White inside, dark red outside, with 5 deeply notched petals; open at dusk and emit a strong scent.
**Distribution:** Fairly common.
**Habitat:** Often found in shady areas among bushes.
**Notes:** Pollinated by moths.

## Honey Heath

*Erica ericoides*
Erica family – Ericaceae

A compact, much-branched, woody **shrub**.
**Leaves:** Small, hairy leaves arranged in 4s.
**Flower head:** Small, honey-scented, rose-pink to whitish, tubular bell-shaped flowers with 4 reddish-brown **anthers** exerted conspicuously beyond the petals. The flowers appear in dense clusters of 6–12 at the top of flower stalks.
**Distribution:** Frequent.
**Habitat:** Lower rocky slopes and flats in the south.

Jan–Apr                    Up to 80cm

## False Slugwort                    Basterslakblom

*Dischisma ciliatum*
Sutera family – Scrophulariaceae

An erect **annual** or **perennial** with a mass of feathery white flowers.
**Leaves:** Narrow, spreading, alternate.
**Flower head:** Numerous small, white flowers emerge from the sides of a tall green flower **spike**, surrounding its upper half with a frilly whiteness.
**Distribution:** Fairly common.
**Habitat:** Upper and lower slopes.
**Notes:** *Hebenstreita cordata* is a lookalike; has red spot-marks on the white flowers.

Aug–Dec                    Up to 40cm

## Flat-topped Bitterbush

*Selago corymbosa*
(Sutera family – Scrophulariaceae)

An erect, densely leaved, sturdy **shrublet** with minutely hairy stems.
**Leaves:** Leaves in tufts, needle-like, spreading, somewhat bottlebrush-looking from a distance.
**Flower head:** Many tiny white flowers with yellow **stamens** cluster on several branchlets to form a dense, flat-topped to rounded **inflorescence**.
**Distribution:** Fairly common.
**Habitat:** Stony flats and slopes.

Dec–May                    Up to 60cm

Sep–Jan | Up to 60cm

# Gerbera

*Gerbera wrightii*
Daisy family – Asteraceae

**A tufted perennial.**
**Leaves:** Dark green, slightly hairy, egg-shaped, softly white-felted below.
**Flower head:** White ray **florets**, sometimes reddish to maroon below, rarely coppery red on both surfaces.
**Bracts** softly felted.
**Distribution:** Rare.
**Habitat:** Lower rocky and grassy sandstone slopes after fires.

Feb–Apr | Up to 30cm

# Grey Pin Buchu

*Macrostylis villosa*
Citrus family – Rutaceae

**An attractive, compact, aromatic shrub with long-lasting white flower clusters.**
**Leaves:** Ascending, overlapping, lance-shaped, short-stalked, hairy or hairless, gland-dotted.
**Flower head:** White or cream flowers in terminal clusters of 11–18 at branch tips, with a beard-like tuft of hairs near the middle of the petals; **stamens** increasingly protrude beyond the flowers with age.
**Distribution:** Frequent.
**Habitat:** Stony mountain areas.

Jul–Nov | Up to 1.2m

# Grey Stilbe

*Stilbe vestita*
Stilbe family – Stilbaceae

**An erect shrub with upright branches and a 'bottlebrush' flower head.**
**Leaves:** Densely crowded, overlapping, needle-like leaves.
**Flower head:** Erect, oval **spike** with fluffy, creamy white flowers, crowded towards top. After flowering, top end of the flower stem remains vertical – resembles a candlestick.
**Distribution:** Occasional.
**Habitat:** Damp sandstone slopes.

## Gunpowder Plant          Kruitbossie
*Silene pilosellifolia*
Carnation family – Caryophyllaceae

An erect to sprawling **perennial** covered with very fine, short, soft hairs.
**Leaves:** Variable, **basal** leaves oval; upper leaves narrow, inversely lance-shaped, stalkless, broadening towards the top.
**Flower head:** White-petalled, deeply notched flowers (rarely purple), widely spaced from each other up a long flower stem. The flowers emerge from a stalkless, long, cyclindrical tube, all facing more or less the same direction.
**Distribution:** Occasional.
**Habitat:** In bushes on lower slopes.

Aug–Jun                    Up to 70cm

## Cinnamon Sambreeltjie
*Hessea cinnamomea*
Amaryllis family – Amaryllidaceae

A bulbous **geophyte** with dark green stems.
**Leaves:** 1–2 **strap-shaped**, shiny, dark green leaves, dry at flowering time.
**Flower head:** Each flowering stalk supports 10–25 glistening white flowers with deep pink to claret or brownish centre. Infrequently, all-red flowers have been found. The flowers are spice scented.
**Distribution:** Rare, often appears after a fire.
**Habitat:** Waterlogged, peaty lowlands.

May–Jun                    Up to 15cm

## Ker-ker
*Erica imbricata*
Erica family – Ericaceae

A distinctive, erect, robust **shrub** with prolific flower-bearing branches.
**Leaves:** Short, in **whorls** of 3 facing upwards.
**Flower head:** Flowers, usually white, with distinctive dark brown **anthers** characteristically protruding. Flowers cluster in 3s (or more) on small, densely leafy, lateral branches and at the ends of upper branchlets.
**Distribution:** Frequent. Widespread.
**Habitat:** Fairly dry, sandy conditions on hills and mountain slopes.
**Notes:** Known as ker-ker because of the sound made when brushing up against the plants.

Feb–Oct                    Up to 50cm

**135**

## Larkspur Baroe                     Fraaibaroe
*Cyphia bulbosa*
Bellflower family – Campanulaceae

**A small, delicate, mauve-white perennial.**
**Leaves:** Few, at base, deeply incised, and well-spaced, getting smaller up the stem.
**Flower head:** Small, funnel-shaped flowers, with flared 2-lipped mouth; occur alternately up the stem.
**Distribution:** Fairly common.
**Habitat:** Upper and lower slopes. Bushy, damp and sheltered areas.
**Notes:** Occurs often after fire.

Aug–Oct                          Up to 40cm

## Little Painted Lady              Vlinderpypie
*Gladiolus debilis*
Iris family – Iridaceae

**An attractive, slender perennial with zigzagging stems.**
**Leaves:** 1–2 lower leaves that can reach almost as high as the stems, and 2 higher leaves, shorter, narrower and thicker.
**Flower head:** 1–3 unscented, white (occasionally pink), long-tubed flowers grow together, each having red arrowhead or spade-like markings on their lower petals (tepals).
**Distribution:** Frequent in specific localities.
**Habitat:** Rocky sandstone slopes on Silvermine plateau.

Aug–Oct                          Up to 50cm

## Little Sundew                   Kleinsnotrosie
*Drosera trinervia*
Sundew family – Droseraceae

**An insectivorous herb.**
**Leaves:** Basal, covered with glandular hairs that secrete sticky fluid; attract and trap small insects that are absorbed by the plant.
**Flower head:** 2–10 small white flowers, each with 5 broad, rounded petals.
**Distribution:** Common.
**Habitat:** Mostly upper slopes, in damp, wind-sheltered areas.

Aug–Sep                          Up to 40cm

## Marsh Daisy Belskruie

*Osmitopsis asteriscoides*
Daisy family - Asteraceae

A tall, sturdy, upright, loosely branched, camphor-scented **shrub**.
**Leaves:** Lower stem leafless; upper stems well-branched with crowded, oval-pointed, hairy leaves.
**Flower head:** Daisy-like flowers, with white petals and a yellow centre, borne towards top of plant on short side branches.
**Distribution:** Common.
**Habitat:** Found in dense stands near streams, **seeps** and in marshy areas.

Aug–Dec      Up to 2m

## Moraea Rietuintjie

*Moraea tricuspidata*
Iris family - Iridaceae

A lovely **cormous geophyte** on an erect, slender stem.
**Leaves:** Single, **basal**, thin, channelled, hairless.
**Flower head:** Distinct white to cream unscented flower, with 3 broad petals, brown-speckled at the centre; borne at the top of a firm, slender stem.
**Distribution:** Fairly common; occasional in Silvermine.
**Habitat:** Lower slopes.
**Notes:** Flowers especially after fires.

Sep–Oct      Up to 60cm

## Mountain Lazybush Sukkelbossie

*Oftia africana*
Sutera family - Scrophulariaceae

A sprawling **shrub** with trailing branches often spreading over, or between, large rocks.
**Leaves:** Stiff, stalkless, narrowly oval, with sharply toothed edges.
**Flower head:** Nondescript white flower with 5 petals and pale green throat; borne, singly, at tips of branches. Chocolate-scented fragrance.
**Distribution:** Common.
**Habitat:** Lower slopes on rocky sandstone and granite.

Jan–Dec      Up to 1m

137

## Mountain Saffronbush

*Gnidia tomentosa*
Daphne family – Thymelaeaceae

A tall, erect, leafy, branching **shrub** with a reddish-brown stem.
**Leaves:** Soft, narrowly oval, pointed, alternate, overlapping, rising up the flowering stem.
**Flower head:** White, trumpet-shaped flower, with 4 small, bright yellow 'petals' standing upright in the centre, flaring at the end in 4 parts.
**Distribution:** Fairly common.
**Habitat:** Upper and lower slopes, often near streams or in damp areas.

Jan–Dec          Up to 1m

## Pelargonium                    Fynblaarmalva

*Pelargonium myrrhifolium* var. *myrrhifolium*
Geranium family – Geraniaceae

A low-growing **perennial** with hairy flower stalks.
**Leaves:** Variable in size, deeply **lobed** or fragmented.
**Flower head:** Up to 6 white flowers, with 2 large upper petals streaked with red veins; well above the leaves.
**Distribution:** Frequently found.
**Habitat:** Often found sheltering under bushes or near stony sand footpaths.
**Notes:** *P.m.* var. *coriandrifolium* is similar but with pinkish-purple flowers and red-edged leaves.

Jan–Dec          Up to 30cm

## Pine-leaved Saffronbush

*Gnidia pinifolia*
Daphne family – Thymelaeaceae

An erect, leafy, single-stemmed **shrub**.
**Leaves:** Short, thin, pine-like, crowded, alternately opposite each other, gradually tapering to a sharp tip.
**Flower head:** 10 or more small, white, tubular flowers, each with 4 petals, clustered in a terminal head at the branch tips. Immature flowers can be pinkish in bud.
**Distribution:** Fairly common.
**Habitat:** Upper and lower slopes.

May–Dec          Up to 1m

## Rose-flowered Sundew      Snotrosie
*Drosera cistiflora*
Sundew family – Droseraceae

A soft, weakly erect, sticky **perennial** with unbranched, leafy stems.
**Leaves:** Slender, stalkless leaves of varying shapes are scattered up the stem. They appear to be hairy and sticky, covered in red or pale hairs with knob-like glands. The **basal** leaves are not always present.
**Flower head:** Large, solitary or few in a terminal **inflorescence**: colours mainly pale rose but can be white, with a dark green to black centre and bright orange **anthers**.
**Distribution:** Common in suitable locations.
**Habitat:** Well-drained slopes or temporary **seeps**.

Aug–Sep      Up to 40cm

## Cluster Spiderhead
*Serruria glomerata*
Protea family – Proteaceae

A compact, rounded **shrub** with feathery foliage and a single, main stem.
**Leaves:** Long, wide, silky-haired leaves, finely divided, curving upwards into cylindrical segments with sharp, fine points.
**Flower head:** Spherically shaped, made up of a mass of tiny flowers crammed together, giving a white, silky look. The flowers are sweetly scented.
**Distribution:** Locally common in Cape Point.
**Habitat:** Sandstone flats and lower slopes.

Jun–Oct      Up to 40cm

## Skunk Bush      Stinkbossie
*Chaenostoma hispidum*
Sutera family – Scrophulariaceae

A small **shrublet** with many erect or sprawling branches.
**Leaves:** Roughly toothed, oval to elliptically shaped; grow in pairs opposite each other.
**Flower head:** White to pink/mauve flowers with a yellow funnel-shaped throat.
**Distribution:** Common.
**Habitat:** Common among bushes on sandy slopes.

Jan–Dec      Up to 50cm

HC

Aug–Nov       Up to 30cm

## Snow Daisy       Wildewitmargriet

*Dimorphotheca nudicaulis*
Daisy family – Asteraceae

A large, **perennial** daisy.
**Leaves:** Long, somewhat ragged, lance-shaped, with toothed edges; crowd the base of the flower.
**Flower head:** Single flowers with gleaming white petals and orange to purple-black centres, on a long, bare flower stalk. Petal undersides are purple to copper-coloured.
**Distribution:** Fairly common.
**Habitat:** Sunny open areas.
**Notes:** *D. pluvialis* is very similar but petal underside is darker and more purple.

CM

Aug–Oct       Up to 25cm

## Cape Buttercup       Botterblom

*Sparaxis grandiflora*
Iris family – Iridaceae

A **cormous geophyte**, branches mainly below ground.
**Leaves:** 6–10 light green, sword-shaped to lance-shaped leaves at the base, sometimes lying on the ground, 2 up the stem.
**Flower head:** The **spike** has up to 5 white to cream-coloured flowers, often with a dark spot in the middle and dark purple swathes on the outer side of the petals.
**Distribution:** Occasional.
**Habitat:** Flats and slopes in renosterveld in the south, or coastal sandveld.

CW

Sep–Oct       Up to 50cm

## Star-eyed Aristea

*Aristea spiralis*
Iris family – Iridaceae

An attractive, erect **perennial** with large flowers.
**Leaves:** Spear-shaped, fairly wide and soft, **sheathing** the flowering stem.
**Flower head:** White (or pale blue) flower has 6 big oval petals with purple markings and orange **anthers**.
**Distribution:** Fairly common.
**Habitat:** Upper and lower slopes, often found in clumps.
**Notes:** Flowers open in the morning, then twist into a spiral as they fade.

## Sticky Heath    Taaiheide
### *Erica physodes*
Erica family – Ericaceae

A sturdy, erect, dense **shrublet** with spreading branches.
**Leaves:** Long, round-pointed leaves.
**Flower head:** Translucent white, small, sticky, balloon-like flowers hang down on little flower stalks in 3s or 4s at ends of side or main branches; they can appear pale greyish-green because of their darker inner **anthers**.
**Distribution:** Occasional.
**Habitat:** Prefers moist western to southwestern rocky upper slopes.
**Notes:** Widespread on Silvermine plateau, south of Constantiaberg.

May–Aug          Up to 70cm


## Stompie
### *Brunia noduliflora*
Brunia family – Bruniaceae

An erect, spreading **shrublet** with moderately hairy branches and ball-shaped flowers.
**Leaves:** Tiny, small, black-tipped, hard-textured, pointed, tightly packed among the stiff branches.
**Flower head:** Creamy white, fluffy balls when young; turn brown around August as the flower dies, then grey-black. Fragrant.
**Distribution:** Occasional.
**Habitat:** Rocky mountain slopes.
**Notes:** Differs from lookalike *Berzelia lanuginosa*, being smaller, more robust, with bigger flowers. Not associated with water.

Jun–Oct          Up to 1.5m


## Sweet Sprayflower    Soetgonna
### *Struthiola dodecandra*
Daphne family – Thymelaeaceae

A graceful, erect **shrub** with wand-like branches.
**Leaves:** Closely packed, small, long, smooth, hairless, faintly ribbed, lance-shaped leaves **sheathe** the erect stem. Leaves opposite, in 4 rows.
**Flower head:** White or pink tubular flowers, with 8 petal-like scales at the mouth, grow up the long stem.
**Distribution:** Locally common.
**Habitat:** Especially seen on mountain slopes in damp areas.

Jun–Mar          Up to 60cm

Oct–Apr     Up to 30cm

## The Mexican

*Erigeron karvinskianus*
Daisy family - Asteraceae

**A pretty, non-indigenous daisy.**
**Leaves:** Light green, narrowly oval, pointed, alternate.
**Flower head:** Daisy-like, with a white, sometimes purple, ring of petals and yellow centre. Grows singly or in small clumps.
**Distribution:** Occasional.
**Habitat:** Mainly southeastern areas along service roads and footpaths.
**Notes:** An immigrant from Mexico, hence its coined name.

Jul–Dec     Up to 50cm

## Rootthug

*Thesium viridifolium*
Sandalwood family - Santalaceae

**A semi-parasitic, much-branched, densely leafy shrublet.**
**Leaves:** Long and narrow, rough edges, low to the ground, bright green when young.
**Flower head:** White flowers in clusters at the top of flower stems, **bracts** nearly the length of the flower.
**Distribution.** Frequent.
**Habitat:** Rocky slopes and flats.
**Notes:** Attaches itself to roots of other plants, hence the common name.

Aug–Oct     Up to 60cm

## Twining Baroe        Bergbaroe

*Cyphia volubilis*
Bellflower family - Campanulaceae

**A small, climbing perennial herb.**
**Leaves:** Slender, hairless, **simple**, lance-shaped, growing from the stem in sets of 3.
**Flower head:** Series of single white flowers, with dark blue **stamens**, on short stems; spaced along the twining shoot. Flowers can also be blue, purple, pink.
**Distribution:** Fairly common.
**Habitat:** Lower slopes, bushy areas.

## Whip-stemmed Featherhead   Katstertjie
*Struthiola ciliata*
Daphne family – Thymelaeaceae

**A tall, thin shrublet.**
**Leaves:** Closely packed, small, lance-shaped, sometimes reddish at their tips; press against and **sheathe** entire erect stem.
**Flower head:** Many small, creamy white (or pink), tubular flowers with 4 squarish petals; flowers emerge, and bend out, from upper sides to top of flower **spike**. Evening scented.
**Distribution:** Frequently found.
**Habitat:** Widespread, upper and lower slopes.

Jan–Dec                    Up to 1.5m

## White Bristle Bush                    Blombos
*Metalasia muricata*
Daisy family – Asteraceae

**A common, erect, rigid, thin-stemmed, multi-branched, densely leaved shrub.**
**Leaves:** Green-grey, lance-shaped, hook-tipped, curving upwards.
**Flower head:** Dull white, woolly, brown underneath, in somewhat rounded clusters at top of branches. Honey-scented.
**Distribution:** Frequently found.
**Habitat:** Widespread, upper and lower slopes.

Apr–Sep                    Up to 2m

## White Harveya                    Witinkblom
*Harveya capensis*
Broomrape family – Orobanchaceae

**An erect, slender, silky-hairy parasitic herb.**
**Leaves:** Small, scale-like, reddish-green.
**Flower head:** Delicate white flowers, which can have a pinkish tinge to the outside of the petals. Buds are pink. Stalkless or short-stalked flowers, each having 5 wavy petals and a yellow-tinged keyhole-shaped throat, grow in a loose terminal arrangement at the top of a stout stem. The flowers are scented at night.
**Distribution:** Occasional.
**Habitat:** Rocky sandstone mountain slopes.
**Notes:** The flowers turn black when dried or pressed and were used by early settlers as an ink, hence the Afrikaans name of 'inkblom'.

Nov–Feb                    Up to 50cm

## White Romulea Witknikkertjie

*Romulea flava*
Iris family – Iridaceae

An erect, **perennial herb**.
**Leaves:** Thread-like, with narrow grooves; taller than the flower.
**Flower head:** White, with 6 petals, yellow cup (throat), on single flower stem.
**Distribution:** Occasional.
**Habitat:** Lower slopes, common in grassy areas.
**Notes:** Yellow form also found but not common.

Jun–Oct    Up to 30cm

## Wild Asparagus Wag-'n-bietjie

*Asparagus rubicundus*
Asparagus family – Asparagaceae

A tall, erect, spiny **shrub** with smooth, glossy, dark reddish-brown, hairless stems that are covered with spreading spines.
**Leaves:** Minute, curved, spine-like leaves are borne on the woody stem and branches.
**Flower head:** Tiny, white, fragrant, long-stalked flowers with 6 drooping petals are widely dispersed about the **shrub**. The flowers give rise to red berries.
**Distribution:** Common.
**Habitat:** Grows on sandy and granite lower slopes, especially to the south and occasionally in wooded areas.

Jan–Jun    Up to 90cm

## Wild Aster Wilde-aster

*Polyarrhena reflexa*
Daisy family – Asteraceae

A straggling **shrub**.
**Leaves:** Small, oblong to lance-shaped, slightly hairy, bending backwards. Leaf edges are scratchy.
**Flower head:** Small daisy flower with white petals, purple-red on reverse, and yellow centre; forms at the end of short stems.
**Distribution:** Fairly common.
**Habitat:** Lower slopes, especially in damp areas.

Jun–Oct    Up to 1m

## Wild Buchu                    Rooiboegoe

*Diosma hirsuta*
Citrus family – Rutaceae

A small, erect, bushy, aromatic **shrublet**.
**Leaves:** Small, narrow, alternate leaves tipped with a short, sharp point.
**Flower head:** Numerous tiny, white, cup-like flowers, with pink-red flower stalks, occur scattered towards the ends of branchlets.
**Distribution:** Fairly common.
**Habitat:** Clay and sandstone slopes.
**Notes:** *D. oppositifolia* is similar – a bigger plant with short leaves in neat rows, each pair alternately opposite. Flowers, mainly in pairs, with green centre.

Apr–Sep                    Up to 50cm

## Wild Clove Bush              Bergklappers

*Montinia caryophyllacea*
Montinia family – Montiniaceae

An erect, thin **shrublet**.
**Leaves:** Blue-green, longish, oblong pointed, alternate, with well-defined mid-vein.
**Flower head:** Somewhat sparse, small, white, 4-petalled flowers at tips of branches.
**Distribution:** Common.
**Habitat:** Mainly lower mountain slopes.

Jun–Dec                    Up to 1.5m

## Wild Rosemary                Kapokbossie

*Eriocephalus africanus*
Daisy family – Asteraceae

An evergreen, multi-branched, twiggy **shrub**.
**Leaves:** Small, narrow, silvery green, hairy, aromatic, in tufts along the branches.
**Flower head:** Small, white flowers, with roughly scalloped petals and reddish-brown centres; form in small clusters at branch tips. Flower head is fluffy or woolly at fruiting time.
**Distribution:** Fairly common.
**Habitat:** Lower, dry, western granitic slopes.
**Notes:** Birds use the fluffy seed heads for nest lining.

Apr–Oct                    Up to 1m

GN

**Jul–Dec**  From 40–80cm

## Wild Tobacco   Wildetabak
*Silene undulata*
Carnation family – Caryophyllaceae

An erect, rather sticky, sprawling **perennial** with distinctly notched petals.
**Leaves:** Long, thin, hairy, lance-shaped, alternately opposite, spaced up the stem.
**Flower head:** White (or pink/red) 5-petalled flower, each petal deeply **lobed** so it looks V-shaped.
**Distribution:** Common.
**Habitat:** In shady places and on slopes.
**Note:** This flower has a short and long form, hence the height range.

CM

**Apr–Nov**  Up to 20cm

## Spike Lily   Witkoppie
*Wurmbea spicata*
Colchicum family – Colchicaceae

A **cormous geophyte.**
**Leaves:** 3-channelled, **basal** leaves up to 20cm long.
**Flower head:** White to cream flowers, almost stalkless, the petals sometimes dark to almost black at the tips; flowering in a dense **spike** at the top of a long, unbranched flowering stem. Wonderfully scented in the evenings.
**Distribution:** Occasional.
**Habitat:** Mostly clay and granite slopes in renosterveld.

FS

**Jun–Oct**  Up to 30cm

## Purple Drumstick Flower  Verfblommetjie
*Zaluzianskya villosa*
Sutera family – Scrophulariaceae

A hairy **annual herb.**
**Leaves:** Stalked or stalkless, opposite, densely hairy, with rough-edged, spoon-shaped leaflets, slightly toothed.
**Flower head:** Pinwheel flowers with 5 Y-shaped petals, white or mauve, or lilac with yellow eyes, turning reddish after pollination occurs, in a compact mass at the tip of flower stem. The plant emits a honey scent at night.
**Distribution:** Frequent.
**Habitat:** Sandy places on flats and low slopes.

## Leek-orchid
### Orgideekie

*Disa bracteata*
Orchid family – Orchidaceae

Sep–Nov     Up to 30cm

An erect, **tuberous perennial**.
**Leaves:** Long, erect, narrow to lance-shaped with sharp pointed tips, tapering from a rounded base toward the apex.
**Flower head:** Many small bicoloured flowers form on each stalk, with hooded red-brown upper sections and greenish-yellow lower parts.
**Distribution:** Frequent.
**Habitat:** Moist, sandy flats and mountains.

## Snake Lily
### Slangkop

*Ornithoglossum viride*
Colchicum family – Colchicaceae

Jun–Sep     Up to 20cm

A **cormous perennial** with some variety in appearance.
**Leaves:** 3–8 lance-shaped, blue-grey leaves, with 2–4 channelled leaves **sheathing** the base, smaller up the stem.
**Flower head:** Bicoloured, green and purple, with yellow **stamens** on long stalks nodding downwards; the long petals bend upward in a crown-like shape.
**Distribution:** Frequent.
**Habitat:** Sandy soil in lower flats and coastal areas.

## Broad-leaved Stork's Bill
### Kaneelbol

*Pelargonium lobatum*
Geranium family – Geraniaceae

Sep–Nov     Up to 50cm

A long-stalked **geophyte** whose flower shape resembles a windmill.
**Leaves:** Large – up to 30cm in diameter, oval-shaped, with ragged edges; lie on ground.
**Flower head:** Many flowers mass in spreading clusters at tips of flower stalks. Each flower has 5 two-tone petals – dark purple-black edged with yellow. Flowers clove-scented at night.
**Distribution:** Occasional.
**Habitat:** Bushy, sunny areas.
**Notes:** *P. triste*, very common in Silvermine, has a similar flower head, but the leaves are different – further up the stem, deeply incised, fragmented and feathery.

Aug–Oct | Up to 80cm

## Spider Lily

Spinnekopblom

*Ferraria crispa*
Iris family – Iridaceae

A thick and pulpy flowering plant (**geophyte**) with multi-branched leafy stems.
**Leaves:** Basal, many, broad, **succulent**, leathery, sword-shaped. Higher up: smaller, overlapping, wrapping round and enfolding each other.
**Flower head:** Starfish-shaped, variably coloured – from treacle-brown to maroon, to dark purple blotches over yellow or cream. Petal edges wavy, crinkled and crisp.
**Distribution:** Rare – found only in a few locations.
**Habitat:** Sandy and rocky areas, lower northeastern slopes.
**Notes:** Foul-smelling and short-lived; attracts flies.

May–Dec | Up to 50cm

## Cat's Tail Bush

Katstert

*Microdon dubius*
(Sutera family – Scrophulariaceae)

A soft, wand-like, branched **perennial** with stems that are minutely hairy.
**Leaves:** Small, thin, narrow, lance-shaped – borne on a reddish-brown, notched, woody stem.
**Flower head:** Tiny, curved, fragrant, 5-**lobed**, tubular-shaped flowers, yellow in colour but often with maroon to brownish petals, are borne on an elongated **spike**. The flowers give off a distinctive sweet scent at night.
**Distribution:** Common.
**Habitat:** On sandstone slopes.

May–Jun | Up to 45cm

## Brown Afrikaner

Bruinafrikaner

*Gladiolus maculatus*
(Iris family – Iridaceae)

A slender **perennial**, generally flowering in Winter.
**Leaves:** 3 or 4 narrow, leathery, short-bladed leaves, 2 **basal**, the lowermost **sheathing** the lower half of the stem. Leafless at flowering time.
**Flower head:** Strongly scented, long-tubed, funnel-shaped, brownish-yellow, with many brown or purple-brown spots. This colouring of the flowers can be very variable, and occasionally the brown pigment is missing, leaving yellow flowers.
**Distribution:** Frequent in localized areas, especially in the south.
**Habitat:** Lower mountain slopes.
**Notes:** Pollinated by moths.

## Hellroot

*Orobanche minor*
Broomrape family – Orobanchaceae

Aug–Nov · Up to 40cm

A **parasite** lacking in green coloration. It obtains all its nutrients from the roots of its host plants, which are mainly members of the Pea (Fabaceae) and Daisy (Asteraceae) families.

**Leaves:** 1–2cm long, sparsely spaced, scale-like leaves, the same colour as the stem, overlapping at the base of stem.
**Flower head:** Unscented tubular flowers in a **spike**, dull brownish-mauve and yellow. The flower stalks are light tan to brown and sometimes purple coloured.
**Distribution:** Commonly widespread, now considered a South African naturalized alien.
**Habitat:** A wide variety of soils: moist, light (sandy), medium (loamy) and heavy (clay) soils.

## Wild Garlic                                    Wildeknoflok

*Tulbaghia alliacea*
Onion family – Alliaceae

Mar–May · Up to 30cm

A stemless, bulbous **perennial** producing **rosettes** of grass-like leaves.

**Leaves:** 3–6, thin and narrow with rounded tip, **strap-shaped**, absent or emergent at flowering, said to smell of onion when bruised.
**Flower head:** 6–10 tubular flowers, yellow-brown petals with an orange mouth, sweetly scented especially at night, at the top of a long flower stalk, nodding downwards, moving in any light breeze.
**Distribution:** Common.
**Habitat:** On flats and sandy lower slopes and on clay and gravel soils.

## Brown Sage                                    Bruinsalie

*Salvia africana-lutea*
Mint family – Lamiaceae

Jul–Jan · Up to 2m

A densely leaved, loosely spreading **shrub**.

**Leaves:** Oval-shaped, pointed, green-grey, aromatic, hairy.
**Flower head:** Unusual flowers: shaped like a parrot's beak and coloured treacle brown. Flowers in profusion, in pairs at branch tips.
**Distribution:** Fairly common.
**Habitat:** Bushy places, often found on sandy soils.
**Notes:** Early European botanists, looking at dried specimens, named the plant 'lutea' (meaning yellow), in the belief that there were no brown flowers.

149

Halfway up Kasteelspoort with Lion's Head in the distance

# GLOSSARY

Terms defined below are used in **bold** in the book. Some terms are illustrated on the opposite page.

**annual:** plant with a life cycle of one year; annuals grow from seed, bloom, produce seeds and die in one year

**anther:** end part of stamen, contains the pollen

**basal:** at, or arising from, the base of the stem

**bracts:** modified leaves often found around base of flower head or rising up and above flowers to look like petals

**compound (leaves):** consisting of two or more separate leaflets – opposite of simple

**cormous:** referring to a corm – an underground, swollen, bulb-like, food-storing stem, sometimes with thin, papery leaves

**floret:** small flower that is part of a larger flower

**fynbos:** fine-leaved, shrub-like vegetation; the unique vegetation of the Cape Floristic Region, such as Proteas, Ericas, etc.

**geophyte:** plant with an underground food-storage organ, such as a bulb

**herb:** plant with one permanent stem, smaller than a shrub, non-woody, usually soft-bodied

**inflorescence:** arrangement of flowers on a plant

**insectivorous (plants):** feeding on insects

**kloof:** Afrikaans word for ravine or valley

**lobed (leaves):** partly divided but not separated

**parasite (plants):** plant that obtains its food from another plant

**perennial:** plant that lives for several years, flowering annually

**rosette:** circular arrangement of leaves opening out from a central part, usually at or near ground level

**seep:** where water seeps out of the ground

**sheathe:** to wrap around and protect, such as a leaf wrapping around a stem

**shrub:** plant with many stems and branches; may grow up to 6m in height (often referred to as a woody plant)

**shrublet:** a small shrub

**simple (leaves):** having a single, undivided blade – opposite of compound

**spike:** an upright, unbranched flower stem from which flowers grow, from the bottom up

**stamen:** male, pollen-producing part of a flower, comprising a stalk (filament) and an anther

**stigma:** female reproductive organ of a flower, receptive to pollen

**strap-shaped/strap-like (leaves):** elongated and flat, like a belt or strap

**style:** stalk arising from the ovary, bears stigma in a position where it can receive pollen

**succulent:** plant with fleshy, swollen stems and leaves that store water

**tuber:** swollen stem or root that stores food and water underground

**tuberous:** referring to a tuber (see above)

**whorl:** ring-like arrangement of similar parts coming from a common point

# ILLUSTRATED GLOSSARY

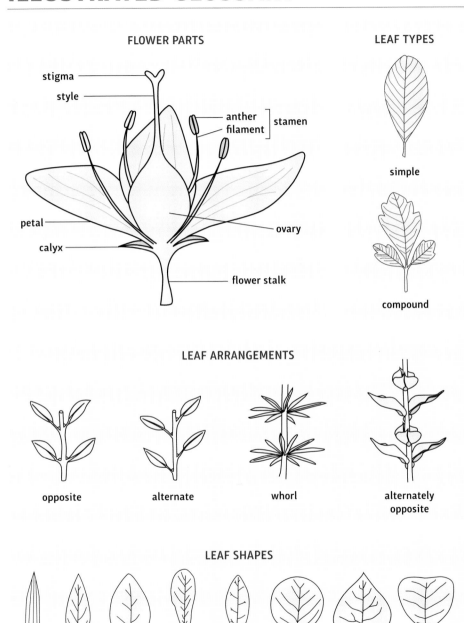

**FLOWER PARTS**

stigma

style

anther
filament } stamen

petal

calyx

ovary

flower stalk

**LEAF TYPES**

simple

compound

**LEAF ARRANGEMENTS**

opposite

alternate

whorl

alternately
opposite

**LEAF SHAPES**

sword    lance    oval    spoon    elliptical    round    triangular    wedge

*Lobostemon montanus* foregrounds a view of Hout Bay from Chapman's Peak

# REFERENCES AND WEBSITES

We would like to acknowledge the use of the following sources when compiling this book:

Bean, A & Johns, A. 2005. *Stellenbosch to Hermanus. South African Wild Flower Guide 5.* Botanical Society of South Africa, Cape Town

Burman, J. 1991. *The Table Mountain Book.* Human & Rousseau, Cape Town

Cowling, R & Richardson, D. 2000 reprint. *Fynbos.* Fernwood Press, Vlaeberg

Fernkloof Nature Reserve website: www.fernkloof.org.za

Goldblatt, P & Manning, J. 2000. *Cape Plants: A conspectus of the Cape Flora of South Africa.* National Botanical Institute of South Africa & MBG Press, Missouri Botanical Gardens, USA

Goldblatt, P & Manning, J. 2000. *Wildflowers of the Fairest Cape.* National Botanical Institute of South Africa & ABC Press, Cape Town

Harris, JG & Woolf, M. 2004. *Plant Identification Terminology.* Spring Lake Publishing, USA

Jackson, WPU. 1977. *Wild Flowers of Table Mountain.* Howard Timmins, Cape Town

Jackson, WPU. 1980. *Wild Flowers of the Fairest Cape.* Howard Timmins, Cape Town

Kesting, D. 2003. *Checklist of the Wild Flowers of the Cape Peninsula.* Friends of Silvermine Nature Area

Manning, J. 2003. *Wildflowers of South Africa.* Briza Publications, Pretoria

Manning, J. 2007. *Field Guide to Fynbos.* Struik Publishers, Cape Town

Manning, J. 2009. *Field Guide to Wild Flowers of South Africa.* Struik Nature, Cape Town

Oliver, I & Oliver, T. 2000. *Ericas of the Cape Peninsula.* National Botanical Institute, Cape Town

Paterson-Jones, C. 1991. *Table Mountain Walks.* Struik Publishers, Cape Town

Rebelo, T. 2000. *Proteas of the Cape Peninsula.* National Botanical Institute, Cape Town

South African National Biodiversity Institute websites: newposa.sanbi.org/sanbi/Explore www.plantzafrica.com www.redlist.sanbi.org

The Plant List website: www.theplantlist.org

Trinder-Smith, T. 2006. *Wild Flowers of the Table Mountain National Park. South African Wild Flower Guide 12.* Botanical Society of South Africa, Cape Town

Tropicos® website: www.tropicos.org

# INDEX

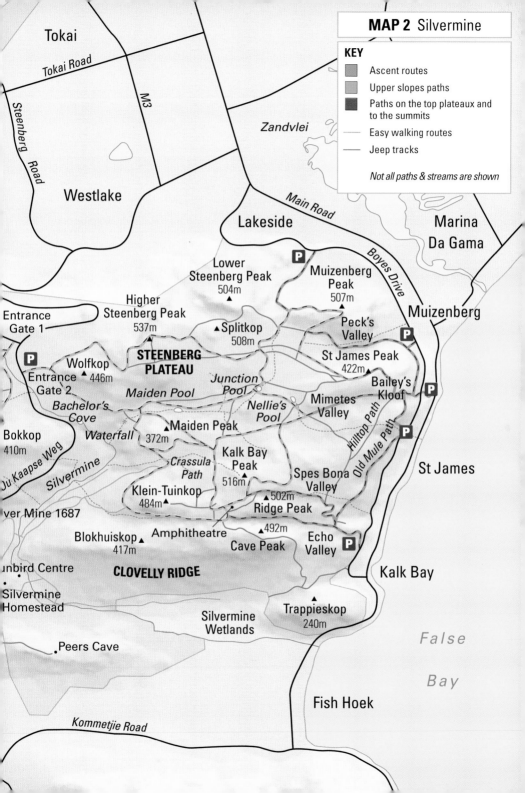

MAP 2 Silvermine

**KEY**

Ascent routes
Upper slopes paths
Paths on the top plateaux and to the summits
Easy walking routes
Jeep tracks

*Not all paths & streams are shown*

Tokai

Tokai Road

M3

Westlake

Steenberg Road

Zandvlei

Lakeside

Main Road

Marina Da Gama

Muizenberg

Boyes Drive

Entrance Gate 1

Higher Steenberg Peak
537m

Lower Steenberg Peak
504m

▲ Splitkop
508m

Muizenberg Peak
507m

Peck's Valley

St James Peak
422m

**STEENBERG PLATEAU**

Wolfkop
▲ 446m

Entrance Gate 2

Maiden Pool

*Bachelor's Cove*

Junction Pool

Nellie's Pool

Mimetes Valley

Bailey's Kloof

Bokkop
410m

Waterfall

▲ Maiden Peak
372m

Ou Kaapse Weg

Silvermine

*Crassula Path*

Kalk Bay Peak
516m

Spes Bona Valley

St James

Hilltop Path

Old Mule Path

ver Mine 1687

Klein-Tuinkop
484m ▲

▲ 502m
Ridge Peak

Blokhuiskop ▲
417m

Amphitheatre

▲ 492m
Cave Peak

Echo Valley

Kalk Bay

unbird Centre

**CLOVELLY RIDGE**

Silvermine Homestead

Silvermine Wetlands

Trappieskop
240m

*False*

*Bay*

Peers Cave

Fish Hoek

Kommetjie Road

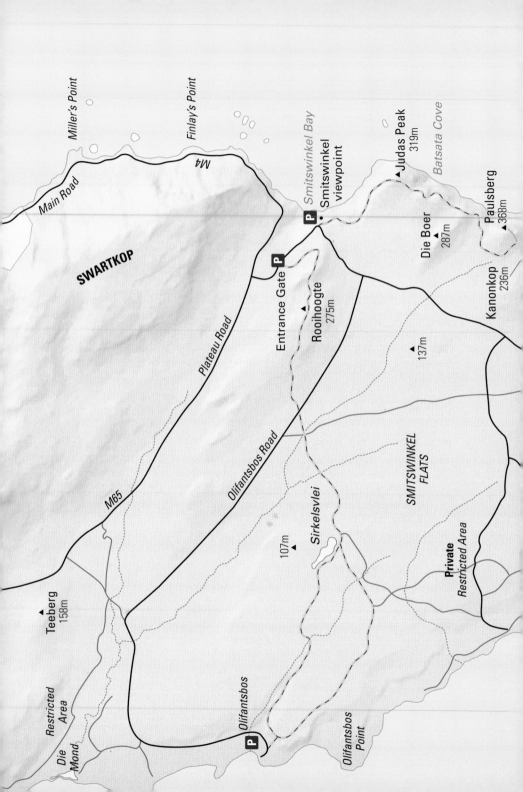